For EU product safety concerns:
IN TECH d.o.o., Prolaz Marije Krucifikse Kozulić 3, 51000 Rijeka, Croatia,
info@intechopen.com or visit our website at intechopen.com.

Meet the editor

Dr. Joceli Mayer graduated in electrical engineering from the Universidade Federal de Santa Catarina (UFSC), Brazil, in 1998. He received a master's degree in electrical engineering from UFSC in 1991 and a master's degree in computer engineering and a doctoral degree from the University of California at Santa Cruz (UCSC), USA, in 1998 and 1999, respectively. He received the Best Student Paper Award from the IEEE International Conference on Image Processing and IBM in 2006 and became an IEEE senior member in 2012. Currently, Dr. Mayer is a full professor of electrical engineering at UFSC. He has published more than 100 articles in conferences and periodicals, authored two books and two chapters, and advised undergraduate and graduate students on research projects. He has developed and supervised projects on super-resolution, speech compression, VOIP systems, image processing, digital watermarking, hard-copy document authentication, and assistive technology applications for hearing-, speech-, and mobility-disabled people with the Internet of Things and speech recognition technologies. His research has been supported by industry and government agencies including FINEP, CNPq, Hewlett Packard, and Intelbras, among others.

Contents

Preface **IX**

Chapter 1 **1**
Information Hiding and Copyrights
by Istteffanny Isloure Araujo

Chapter 2 **23**
Recent Advances in Steganography
by Mahmud Ahmad Bamanga, Aliyu Kamalu Babando and Mohammed Ahmed Shehu

Chapter 3 **45**
Steganography: Unveiling Techniques and Research Agenda
by Arvind Kumar Op Dangi, Stuti Tandon, Shalesh Deorari and Rajeev Kumar

Chapter 4 **69**
A Deep Dive into Reversible Adversarial Examples
by Jiayang Liu and Jun Sakuma

Chapter 5 **83**
Combining Learning Algorithms with Explainable AI to Assess the Strength of Steganography Passwords
by V. Balaji and P. Selvaraj

Chapter 6 **101**
Encryption Scheme for the Security of Digital Images Based on Josephus Traversal and Chaos Theory
by Manzoor Lone

Chapter 7 **115**
Perspective Chapter: Quantum Steganography – Encoding Secrets in the Quantum Domain
by Arun Agrawal, Rishi Soni and Archana Tomar

Chapter 8 **131**
Network Covert Channels
by Muawia Elsadig

Preface

This book provides a selection of chapters on the subject of steganography. Steganography is the practice of undetectably altering a digital work to embed a message. The undetectability of the message in the altered work is an essential property of steganography, whereas the required alterations in the work may be perceived as long as the hidden information is undetectable and therefore also undecipherable by nonauthorized parties. The design of a steganographic algorithm concerns the properties of the communication medium or channel; the cover work, usually in digital format; and the functions of embedding and decoding the message. As cybersecurity becomes increasingly essential to communications worldwide, hidden or undetectable communication provided by enhanced steganography techniques enables the secure information sharing required by many applications. For business, governmental, or personal sharing of information via communication networks, countermeasures need to be taken to ensure that a third party is unable to detect the existence of a message embedded in the work and to avoid even attempts at decode the information without authorization of the sender. The property of undetectability of steganography along with cryptographic techniques has derived secure information schemes in the literature and has been applied in practice. The issues and properties of steganography have been investigated by scientists and practitioners in order to evolve techniques to improve security while sharing information in the open network.

This book offers chapters on steganography ranging from definitions to the basics issues and properties, scientific research on diverse techniques, applications for a variety of areas (cybersecurity, military or defense, law enforcement, healthcare, financial services, etc.), and discussions on future applications and current research on the topic. The chapters provided in this book include "Information Hiding and Copyrights" by Istteffanny Isloure Araujo; "Recent Advances in Steganography" by Mahmud Ahmad Bamanga, Aliyu Kamalu Babando, and Mohammed Ahmed Shehu; "Steganography: Unveiling Techniques and Research Agenda" by Arvind Kumar Op Dangi, Stuti Tandon, Shalesh Deorari, and Rajeev Kumar; "A Deep Dive into Reversible Adversarial Examples" by Jiayang Liu and Jun Sakuma; "Combining Learning Algorithms with Explainable AI to Assess the Strength of Steganography Passwords" by V. Balaji and P. Selvaraj; "Encryption Scheme for the Security of Digital Images Based on Josephus Traversal and Chaos Theory" by Manzoor Lone; "Perspective Chapter: Quantum Steganography – Encoding Secrets in the Quantum Domain" by Arun Agrawal, Rishi Soni, and Archana Tomar; and "Network Covert Channels", by Muawia Elsadig.

We invite the readers to embark on this journey to discover or improve knowledge on the topic of steganography provided by the diversity of chapters in this book.

Joceli Mayer, Ph.D.
Electrical and Electronics Department,
University Federal de Santa Catarina, UFSC,
Florianopolis, Brazil

Chapter 1

Information Hiding and Copyrights

Istteffanny Isloure Araujo

Abstract

This chapter explores the use of steganography on digital files and produces an enhanced technique that addresses the major vulnerabilities that make algorithms less reliable in securing data. Through a review of historical techniques in the field, the study identifies weaknesses in the algorithms to improve security and increase capacity using different techniques. One of the approaches proposed in this study involves a distributed method, which is simple, clear, low-cost, and agile. The study also analyses data manipulation and embedding processes in different files and for different purposes, such as vulnerabilities or placeholders exploited by criminals distributing viruses over the internet using Steganography. The results of the study can help forensic analysts identify secret content and raise awareness about protecting against eavesdropping data on devices. The study proposes a new scheme to improve Steganography called DSoBMP, together with guideline materials that have been published in four international peer-reviewed journals, including Springer and used as a stepping stone to collaborate in a worldwide book publication.

Keywords: forensics, information hiding, steganalysis, steganography, cryptography

1. Introduction

There is evidence that information hiding plays a pivotal role in regulating confidentiality in Cybersecurity. Steganography is a major area of interest within the field of Information hiding. Recently researchers have shown an increased interest in Copyrights. The main challenge faced by many researchers is the weaknesses of current algorithms to protect copyright data and issues such as low capacity to embed the information hiding or logarithm of copyrights to digital data files. Data from several studies suggested that capacity, detectability and distortion are the main issues in terms of using information hiding to protect copyright materials. A much-debated question is whether you can improve one area without compromising the other. Previous studies of information hiding have limited content and considerations with Big Data or even with studying different digital data files that can lead to a stronger technique. Up to now, too little attention has been given to improving all weaknesses of Steganography at the same time and in different files. Currently, there is no data on how to effectively stop applications such as snipping tools in all files, using different applications. This chapter deals with improvements of the main weaknesses of Steganographic Information hiding on different files using a combination of techniques and a distributive approach, we name this method Distributed Steganography over BMP phase I (DSoBMP-I) even though we can use it on different data files, the conversion to BMP type can increase capacity and improve many areas of Steganographic methods, such as flexibility to use it within other file formats. The specific objective of this research is to use intellectual property materials and apply copyrights. A qualitative and Quantitative research design was adopted, providing new insight into the distribution of the copyright content using a safer method that increases capacity, lowers detectability and minimizes distortion. The reader should bear in mind that still there are vulnerabilities within snipping tools and print screen techniques to be analyzed further. The experience of working with photographic content and social media led to the idea of applying a strong copyright that would follow the creative content without being easily broken by cyber criminals. The first session will examine file structures and information hiding applied to them, followed by recent work, copyright issues and the DSoBMP method and its implications.

2. Steganographic file structure exploits programmatically

Many information hiding methods are essential to either secure copyrights or identify malicious data embedded in files, like checking content on the end of the file tags on PDF documents - EOF or EOI at the end of the image files, plus checking on metadata for any other format - the description of the file, programmatically as well as the size of the file. False-positive events, meaning that there is no malicious content, simply a secure message or an error from the program are also valuable information to consider when trying to identify hidden content. The study of software that identifies malicious data is beneficial to understanding how to protect confidential information and copyrights, but it is difficult to get hold of the original code to reverse engineer it. It would be unsafe to disseminate it, as if cybercriminals get access, they could potentially uncover secret messages, see **Figure 1** for the File chunks, containing EOF and EOI to hide data.

We are not primarily focused on using steganalysis to identify crimes. Instead, we analyze and use the best carrier (image file format) along with Distributed Steganography to ensure the security of private messages and copyrights. Our proposed method of Distributed Steganography involves embedding confidential data over several different images generated from the original carrier of the stego-image. This technique provides a successful steganography tool to share images on the web without infringing on the author's copyrights [1]. We approach this method differently, as shown in **Figure 2**.

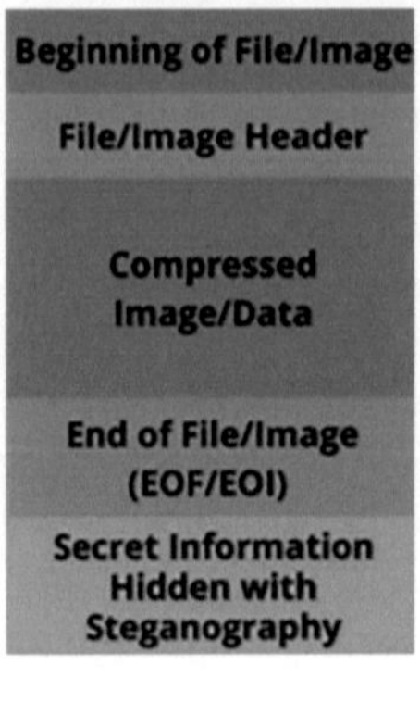

Figure 1.
EOF/EOI capabilities of hiding data.

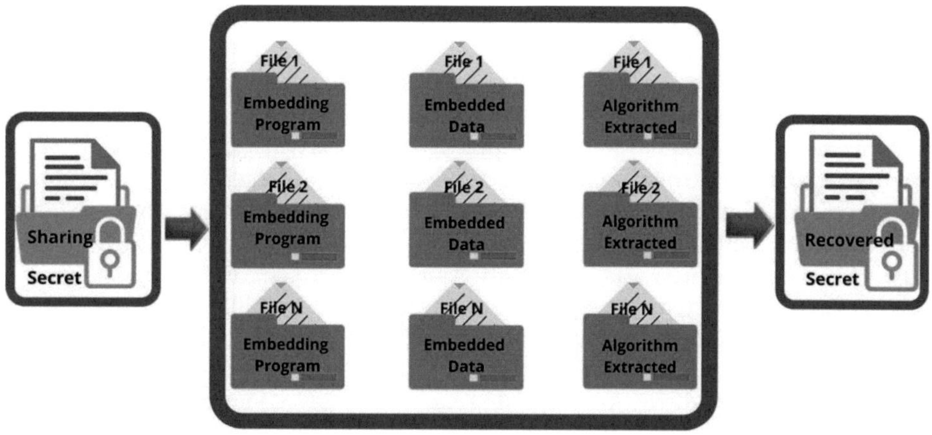

Figure 2.
Distributed steganography.

An image can be represented as a matrix of pixels, and the Spatial Domain of an image is simply the image itself. Image Steganography techniques that use the Spatial Domain method modify the pixel values of an image, but such techniques are not foolproof and can be vulnerable to steganalysis [2]. Private Key Steganography, on the other hand, involves using a key to embed and extract data [3]. It is possible to have the key generated automatically, eliminating the need for manual selection. However, dealing with different file formats and image structures can be complex. **Figure 3** demonstrates the stages involved in a JPEG-based technique, and each stage involves various algorithms and tasks, adding to the overall complexity [4].

The capacity of steganography algorithms refers to the amount of data that can be hidden within a carrier file, which in our case is an image while adhering to the limitations of the particular algorithm [5]. Capacity is also used to detect steganography in an image, as heavily modified bits can indicate the presence of hidden data. Therefore, capacity is a key metric for measuring the effectiveness of steganography algorithms.

Structure of a file Compressed

SOI	Start of Image
APP1	Application Maker 1 (Exif Info)
APP2	Application Maker 2 (FlashPix data)
DQT	Define Quantization Table
DHT	Define Huffman Table
DRI	Define Restart Interval
SOF	Header of Frame
SOS	Start of Scan
	Data Compressed
EOI	End of Image

APP1 Structure

Maker of APP1
Length of APP1
Identifier Code for Exif
Header of TIFF (Tagged Image File Format) – could be 8x bigger than JPEG
0th IFD (Image File Directory)
1st IFD
1st IFD Value
1st IFD Data Image

Figure 3.
Structure of JPEG.

Digital files with lower capacity tend to have higher detectability [6]. To understand the capacity of a file or image, we need to study the structure in detail. The structure of a JPEG file has its complexity and embedded compression techniques, they are not very proficient with Steganalysis. Algorithms with low capacity tend to introduce more distortion to steganographic files. That is why research on ways to improve capacity while minimizing detectability and distortion is highly valuable, given the significant impact these factors have on each other. Encryption can render a message unreadable by encrypting some or all of it, while Watermarking is used to add visible copyright messages, and Encryption is used to secure them invisibly.

Achieving higher capacity without compromising detectability and distortion is a challenging task indeed. It is important to conduct a steganalysis investigation to detect the presence of steganography. While there are several methods to detect steganography, observing distortion is the simplest way to do so. **Figure 4** shows different Steganalysis techniques such as visual, statistical, signature-based, spread spectrum and transform domain. Visual techniques are the most commonly used ones. If there is visible distortion, it becomes easier to determine if there is content hidden inside a file, however, visible distortion can also appear on images that are not formatted properly [7]. Therefore, combining more Steganalysis methods provides a better diagnosis. It is worth noting that some algorithms may have minimum distortion but still be detectable through statistical analysis.

The Least Significant Bits (LSB) algorithm is a technique used to hide data in a carrier file without affecting its quality. The hidden content is placed in the least significant bits of the file, which generally does not distort the file. However, the amount of data that can be hidden depends on the LSB capacity of the file. To detect the hidden data, a mathematical Steganalysis algorithm can be used. The LSB method is the most commonly used technique in the Spatial Domain category [8]. It can be used with any file format, but the detection process involves statistical analysis which begins by analyzing the spaces present in the file [9]. Mondal and Mandal's [10] experiments demonstrated how simple it is to hide information in the least significant bits. An example is shown in **Figure 5**. Histogram-based data hiding is a technique that involves inserting data into the highest frequency bits of an image. This method increases the image's robustness and can be reversible since it distributes personal data among the pixels with the highest frequency intensity. The process involves analyzing the intensity of the pixels within a black-and-white or color image, measuring their RGB values (red, green, and blue), as well as their brightness and contrast [11].

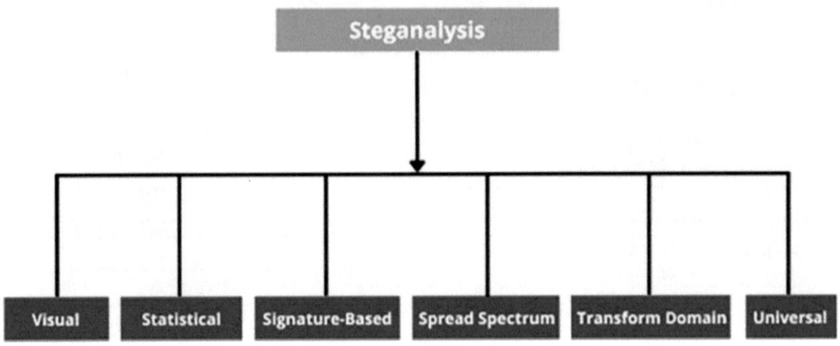

Figure 4.
Steganalysis techniques.

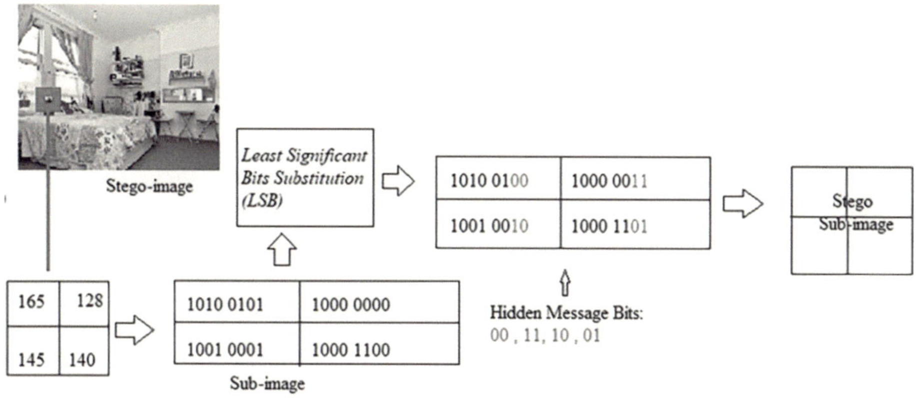

Figure 5.
LSB substitution on images.

By hiding data in specific colors and intensities of a stego image, the technique makes it possible to conceal personal information in a way that is difficult to detect.

The use of the Frequency Domain as a Steganographic technique involves processing the carrier image based on its transform, utilizing mathematical operations to refer to signals by frequency as depicted in **Figure 6**. This approach enhances data security by modifying the image through a variety of techniques outlined below, resulting in a distinct image containing embedded hidden data. Factors such as greyscales, content frequency, and specific methodology are taken into account [12].

The Discrete Cosine Transform (DCT) method is commonly used to compress data on images and videos. This process quantizes the frequency of the data and embeds confidential information in the coefficients. However, this may result in images that are sometimes black and white with limited capacity. The method transforms the values of a pixel in spatial domains into coefficients of the frequency domain. Depending on the sub-method used, the image quality may decrease, leading to visual distortion and detectability due to the hidden data [13].

The Discrete Wavelet Transform in numerical analysis is a wavelength transform that simplifies waves, capturing both frequency and time information [14]. The Discrete Fourier Transform method uses a prime even function without complex numbers for statistics and signaling processing [15]. **Figure 6** shows where this

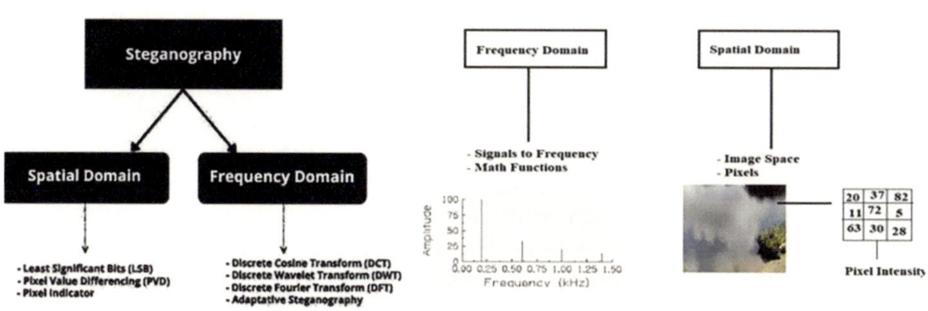

Figure 6.
Frequency vs. spatial domain approach and techniques.

technique belongs among other methods. It involves converting a finite number of equally spaced samples of a function of ordered frequency.

The Adaptive Steganography method utilizes the Human Visual System (HVS) [16]. HVS aims to protect data within pixels less noticeable to humans [17]. Multiple Steganographic methods can be combined to create a sophisticated algorithm that goes unnoticed by humans while embedding secret data into stego images [18]. This method is a mixture of techniques where DCT/LSB applies. It is a combination of DCT and LSB, but it takes into consideration statistical global features. We explored Spatial and Frequency Domains to enhance our method.

The Model-Based method (MB1) embeds information in specific blocks of the image, but it can be easily detected. In contrast, the Block Complexity Data Embedding method (ABCDE) uses watermarks and embeds information at edges. Another approach involves using areas of noise and studying binary patterns that are ignored by the human eye, such as specific colors of the image, like blue [19]. The confidential data is distributed using more than one image and a secret key that is exchanged between the communicating parties [20]. The technique used to hide security data involves splitting it into multiple images, which increases the capacity to hide the data while reducing the footprint. This method aims to prevent unauthorized parties from intercepting the content, as companies must protect their information assets and intellectual property from security breaches. Keeping sensitive data safe is crucial for maintaining a good reputation and avoiding cybercriminals who may exploit vulnerabilities in the device's operating system to view and gather sensitive information. The Frequency Domain Technique is the most reliable framework used for this purpose. However, other commonly used techniques result in a significant increase in image size and distortion when data is hidden, limiting their capacity and increasing detectability.

2.1 The DSoBMP research impact method proposed

Research identifies three major weaknesses of current steganographic algorithms, namely low capacity, high detectability, and distortion. To address these weaknesses and improve data security, a new technique is proposed that focuses on enhancing the capacity of steganography by using multiple carriers. This ensures better protection of data, reduces detectability by embedding data among different images instead of just one, distributes data evenly, and minimizes distortion. The impact of this technique is higher security and protection of steganography algorithms that are used for purposes like copyrights and database security.

The following topics cover essentials that complement the analysis evaluation of current Steganography exploits in this report to prototype the new DSoBMP framework and to test different techniques from current papers using methodologies such as AC Coefficients, ACDCT, Adobe JavaScript, Adobe PostScript, Adobe XML, Metadata Analysis, TJ Spaces Analysis, Arithmetic behind Techniques, Compression for easy hiding, Cover Generation, Cover Stego Attack, Distortion Dynamic-Analysis and Detectable Pattern, Message – Cover Stego Attack, Message Stego Attack, Predicting and Extraction JavaScript, PRNG, Software's to hide data, Spread Spectrum, Statistical Analysis/Anomaly Detection, Stego only Attack, Structural Analysis, Substitution, Substitution of Bytes using XOR and Transform Domain.

The proposed technique offers several advantages over existing approaches. The DSoBMP framework, which is distributed in nature, increases the capacity and decreases detectability and distortion. Additionally, the technique uses the best carrier file to embed data and hides the data using multiple layers of security. This is achieved by using virtually more images originating from the cover medium on the application. The extra partitions on each image are devoted to hiding more information, making it harder to find confidential data since they are randomly distributed in different files. Comparing this technique with LSB alone, which uses one file and any image type, the data is easily found by looking for the least significant bits of the one image for traces of information hidden on LSBs. The main disadvantage is that the technique focuses on BMP, but BMP offers the most capacity increment. However, there is also an improvement in using other image types with distributed steganography. The proposed algorithm is complex and difficult to develop due to the fragments of the file and the data distribution, but complexity in cryptography has always been known to add more security.

2.2 Guide on information about recent work published and gap

The goal of this study was to enhance the security of Steganography techniques through the development of a new framework and algorithm prototype. The purpose of this was to safeguard sensitive data by addressing the weaknesses found in current methodologies. The inspiration for this project came from the identified vulnerabilities of various methods such as Discrete Cosine Transform, which suffer from low capacity, high distortion, and detectability issues and [21] improvements were necessary to address certain issues. Steganography was being used for both positive and negative purposes even before the advent of computers. However, our focus is on using it for the greater good - for protection and security. **Figure 7** explains some of the formal techniques involved in this process. To understand how such attacks listed in the image below can be accomplished, one needs to understand more about computer networks and how the processes of scanning, Accessing and Monitoring can be done in the background with steganography [22].

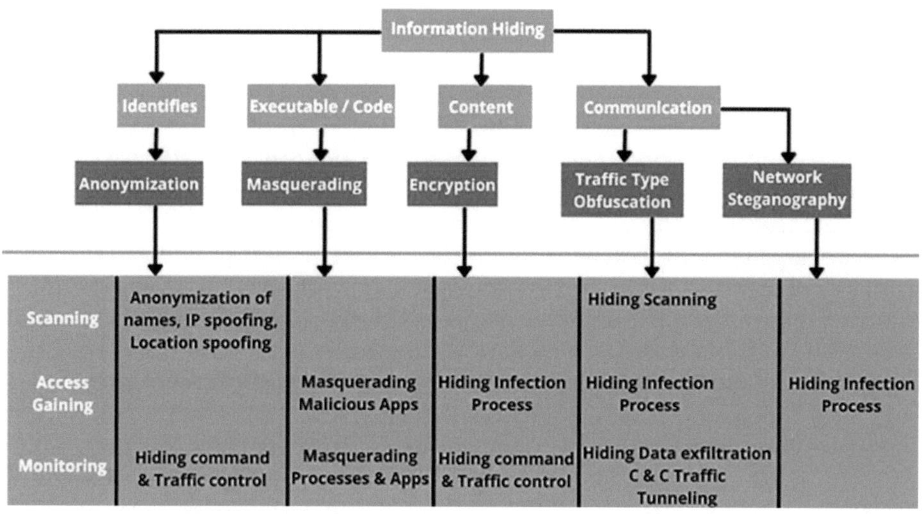

Figure 7.
Formal techniques of steganography.

2.3 Big data, capacity issues and copyright applications

The main task is to address low capacity, high detectability, and distortion in Steganography algorithms. The produced algorithm hides the data among multiple images using BMP as BMP has the purest uncompressed bits that denote higher capacity than other images. By doing that we are maximizing the capacity in two diverse ways, one is by using BMP, which has better capabilities for Steganography, and the second is by using the distributed approach with more images. The structure of BMP is better than other images as the bits are more pure, and uncompressed. The contribution to knowledge is the improvement of the capacity, detectability and distortion using BMP, distributed steganography on Steganographic algorithms. Our research on steganographic algorithms identified weaknesses in popular techniques related to capacity, detectability, and distortion issues. To address these weaknesses, we analyzed existing methodologies and attempted to improve upon them through simulations, measurements, comparisons, and analysis. While many techniques have been used for centuries to secure data, the ever-increasing amount of data requires steganographic algorithms with larger capacity and increased distortion. However, as these methods become more popular, they also become more detectable, necessitating the continuous study and improvement of known methodologies in conjunction with our proposed method.

Cybercriminals put in enormous effort to find the weaknesses of a system, and they release their malicious activities slowly while taking note of how far they can reach. They are also trying to be safe, if not safer than the system, and that is why they succeed. Their success depends on hacking without being noticed, and most of them reach this level quickly. To be secure, we must make sure the data is visible to intended users only, and never let it leak, and if it leaks, we should be able to detect and stop it without damaging the database.

Another point here is the fact that prioritizing the most critical data is essential. In the same way, we restrict employees, for example, by applying access privileges to gain access to some parts of the system as data need to have stringent controls with strong password protection, which is the starting point for protecting the information. It would be great to have 100% security, but it would impact accessibility. The password itself needs to be protected using encryption to hide the passwords from criminals. The algorithm chosen for encrypting the password is crucial. Some algorithms failed on various occasions because of weakness. In later stages, we measure and compare the power of other algorithms including the proposed one as well as other simulations. To provide a good comparison we also consider different files such as different image formats in later exercises that demonstrate the concept of best carriers for Steganographic algorithms in terms of image files.

Some companies still do not encrypt the whole database, instead, they focus on strategy parts to encrypt, like the passwords, and applying other security controls for protection, but any area left unprotected can lead to a security breach. It is essential to perform a backup when dealing with data. If the data leaks and is lost, there must be a plan on how to recover it quickly or have a failover server that will act seemingly. The world today is demanding agile applications and responses, therefore, it is important to dedicate time to risk analysis, risk assessment and recovery plans. Back-up of Big Data has specialized companies that back up in the cloud, mostly a standard for Big Data, these companies also provide disaster recovery to the business these are called Security as a Service, a special area of cloud computing.

Threats are sometimes articulated by people who have intimacy with the system and are otherwise, trusted by the company. It is difficult to find the responsible quickly enough before a data breach. Information Security professionals set up alerts to identify threats, they do identify many indeed if they are watching, but they must act quickly to protect the data while disarming the bomb and then trying to identify the responsible at the same time.

The priority of the Information Security Team in this scenario is to keep all data safe and overcome conflict without damage. We lose control of the data which have leaked, but the data remaining must be protected. If an infected area of the server is affected (the whole server), for example, we might need to take the remaining data out, starting from the most fragile, as in the Crowd Data Scenario, it will take time to transfer everything at once. In the worst-case scenario, transference is a good strategy. If it has a trustful environment, it can be used by whoever is entitled to it and extracted without loss of data control. In the scenario where we leave some data vulnerable as we prioritize to protect sensitive data, we are also taking a risk that can lead to damage, and it would be ideal to have control of where each piece of data is located and get them all safe, controlled and reachable.

It is hard to ensure the owner is tagged to take control of data and ensure ownership. Sometimes this data is lost, and we do not know if the data is used elsewhere, if the new holder applied any security control to override intellectual property, or if the original owner will still be referenced, this is an issue with Crowd-Sourced Data.

Since we are moving to Big Data, and most companies have more than one database to protect, sometimes it is expensively unmanageable for some companies to keep on top of the issue of low capacity and security. Capturing logs is important for identifying issues with behaviors and patterns to analyze data for later working on problem management for investigating eavesdropping, but there are many logs to review, so planning for Big Data is essential as storage capacity is limited and overcrowding a server would slow it down plus it could even crash. An idea is to inbuilt security in each data perhaps using Artificial Intelligence, for location and user interaction logs, but ethical issues must be considered for extracting third-party data and sending information back to the owner, giving automated control and also increasing the amount of memory needed for a system.

Images are copied by thousands of people and used in unusual ways. It is worthwhile having control of intellectual property data logs and data manipulation even as a business idea to monetize the service from the imagined charging peruse and depend on the constraints of different files. Still, we need to consider criminals hacking this model by using screenshots and snipping tools to copy the image, and this can be dealt with by applying law enforcement and making Software have controls on images copied by these means to avoid this intrusive technique.

Moreover, as technology evolves so do hackers. They would attempt to break this system to copy images somehow, and digital Forensics investigators to analyze digital crimes, searching for evidence and presenting proofs of findings, such as how the crime was made possible. It is challenging to crowdsource security and expect only that it becomes more powerful when in fact, sometimes the platform can become more vulnerable as anyone could have access to it and exploit it unless security control and software implementation make use of abstraction methods to customize unique needs and use the trust scenario, where individuals who have contributed in the right way more times get a higher trust certification.

We should not underestimate the fact that ethical hacking, analyzing and mapping paths, and dealing with new threats can lead to better data security, maintenance, and increased security controls. Ethical hacking and Security Audits to find and overcome vulnerabilities ensure data security. Different versions of system bugs fixed increase security, updates play an enormous role in cybersecurity, and using violated software without fixing bugs compromises security.

To protect the data, we need security in-depth, applying security controls and a backup. Capturing a mapping of the data logs to understand where it was visualized in case leakage is necessary, but we must remember to stop snipping Software used to break this pattern to control data copied via applications. The idea of crowdsourcing security could work if individuals were more trustworthy. IT Forensics Examiners should have good technology to identify criminals, the prevention team should be constantly vigilant on alerts and networking monitoring to avoid crimes and capture criminals' tools to protect our confidential or copyright data.

Steganography plays a crucial role in Information Security because it can be applied to all digital files and the issue with privacy and ownership over the web demands awareness of cybercriminals and safe internet usage. Because Steganography will hide the content on the file itself, not requiring the transmission to be highly secure, copyright security applications of digital files such as images, video and audio are one of the main purposes of Steganography algorithms. Without strong security for intellectual property and copyright data, content piracy steals from creative personnel and the industry of software, movies, books music and other content which lose a substantial amount of money to cybercriminals with large-scale copies that are not authorized to circulate on the web, making publishers one of the top clients of securing data using Steganography [23] to embed a hidden message into the archive carrying the digital rights and enabling only authorized people to have certain permissions as in **Figure 8** containing a typical copyright example where images have the details of the owner embedded.

The "invisible" serial number technique and watermarks embed secret data in the files to secure it, banks have started to analyze this approach further to secure confidential data and accounts. The consumer or criminal might not even be aware that these security measures are embedded, and these secret measures can also be used to collect logs which are so important to troubleshoot eavesdropping on attacks over some time as opposed to an attack that is accomplished in a single day.

Encryption can also be used, but the industry finds it beneficial to protect content by concealing it with Steganography for copyrights as unnoticeable marks to avoid

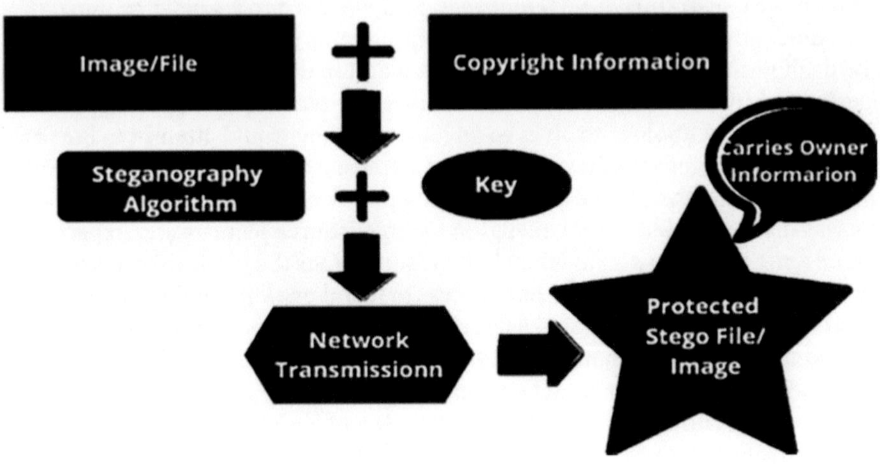

Figure 8.
Typical copyright example.

copies and unauthorized distribution with techniques such as discrete technique per example, to pass as non-existent for the "hacker" [24]. While watermarks denote ownership to the author or company that uses the software, they can also indicate if a document was compromised as different watermark techniques are set to disappear if the document is changed known as the fragile marking method or they are attached to the document in a way that removing would make the data useless.

If a watermark is added to the whole document, the only way to remove it would be by deleting part of the document, hence it could become unreadable as software and if part of the software is deleted to remove the mark, the software would not work as expected or it would be missing features. This method is known as robust marking. Using, the fingerprint method would let the company know exactly who has attempted to modify or distribute the content of an application or a file illegally [25].

2.3.1 Considerations prior DSoBMP

Distributed Steganography is a newer Method using the distribution of data on file(s) and a mix of methods and algorithms. The INFOSEC Convention gave us a few ideas of contemporary issues real companies are dealing with. E.g., the damage of downtime and how attacks that only a few thirty minutes can have a significant impact on the company and if the host companies are at risk, so are we [26]. Focusing on embedding, we researched double embedding and how data extraction does not depend on decryption when reversing data hidden in encrypted images [27].

Also, we studied how vital is Steganography to protect privacy and copyrights, so the original content does not leak or it is lost [28] as well as some crucial terminologies used in Steganographic techniques such as Stego-key that assist in controlling access or recovering the data for people that are aware of its existence, it simply means password and Steganos which is a Stego data containing a hidden message [29] and the converted channel which is the channel of the communication between the sender and the receiver. This is not just used for the transferal of the information data, but it adds extra purposes. We gathered the importance of Steganalysis Software to detect malicious applications and attempt to extract data embedded in the Software to study further to embed data into data [30]. We analyzed how to encrypt the data embedded, so the data is safer inside the file. E.g., embedding the data and then encrypting or encrypting and then embedding [31].

We initiated the research concentrating on the best techniques to embed data so it would be not detected and not extracted or decrypted as one of the definitions of embedding is to make it invisible and undetectable [32], making it a true steganography approach. Plus, if we wish to decrypt, and detect, we should know the best tools and framework for data extraction [33]. We started by researching several techniques such as Cover Generation, Distortion, Spread Spectrum, Statistical, Substitution and Transform Domain, to embed data into an image. We also studied various types of attacks that can be used such as Cover-Stego Attacks, Message-Cover Stego Attacks, Message-Stego Attacks and Stego-only Attacks. We focused on Frequency Domain techniques since it has been the most reliable framework for embedding data into an image. Spatial Domain techniques are not as strong and can be easily detected by Steganalysis [34]. After testing various algorithms, we observed that image size increases when data is hidden. Consequently, we looked into methods of hiding data without increasing size, we were able to simulate all algorithms using one program to test the different algorithms and experiment with different file types. We have different languages from which we simulated techniques, e.g., Python, which seemed incredibly attractive as it is a faster development. The result would be the same independent of the language used, like Java, and JavaScript as the emphasis is always the proof of concept and functionality as opposed to design and beauty. The main task during the experimental phase was digitizing, simulating and testing existing algorithms. By doing that, it was possible to emphasize the creation of a new one with enhancements.

2.4 Protecting copyright with enhanced steganography on images

This method is used to understand how to combat eavesdropping using Steganography, enhancing it to use as a protection technique analyzing studies on both eavesdropping and Steganography defense and how to add copyrights. After understanding how device infection happens with practical experiments, the details gathered reinforce how to identify the steganography practice, highlighting weaknesses in identifying eavesdropping on the device, so we can finalize by developing ways of preventing this interception and enhancing the technique.

We make sure that the developed measure works on mobile devices in general and not just one type of Operating System hence PDFs and Image Files are an excellent approach to follow. This path also takes into account how to use Steganography to combat eavesdropping and protect copyright materials; therefore, this new path involves researching current methods to improve Steganography and use it to benefit security. For this reason, the initial investigation involved eavesdropping and simulating Steganography techniques concurrently to prevent it from being used maliciously not just on phones, but on all devices and also enhancing it for security purposes.

To protect personal photos and copyright materials, using the DSoBMP framework prototype to enhance security, one approach is to add one Steganographic image file that later can be added to a PDF or other document or software with the details of the owner/software to protect a database system, DVD, CD, and any other digital material. To secure and separate the information from the original file, a few carrier images are created from the provided image file, diverting the attention of any interceptor from the actual carriers. The original image is believed to have a stego-image, but its transformed parts contain the data to be protected. This technique can increase the storage capacity by using fragmented images to embed the data, making it a better method for carrying more important data like databases.

The technique also reduces the chances of detection by partitioning the image into different layers and generating a new set of images that are used as the carrier for the content. This prototype methodology named DSoBMP-I (Distributed Steganography over BMP phase I) application has enhanced the security by decreasing detectability perception and increasing the capacity of the original carrier. It has been found that BMP provides the best security and capacity compared to other file formats such as PNG and JPEG. After conducting various tests, we found that BMP was the most reliable format for enhancing capacity and security. We will discuss the results of these tests in detail in the next chapter. We also applied encryption to the hidden data to add an extra layer of security. We analyzed different encryption techniques and found the best approach for our chosen file format. The Frequency Domain technique was the first technique we analyzed as it is the most commonly used. We also looked at the Discrete Cosine Transform (DCT) method for vulnerabilities and found room for improvement. We included round-off error checks when converting to this format.

The BMP file format is a type of image file that contains a map of bits stored as an array of bytes. Unlike other image formats like JPEG, BMP does not use compression.

Instead, it stores all the bytes of the image. Compression techniques like JPEG are used to reduce the file size of digital images. To work with BMP files effectively, it is crucial to have a good understanding of their structure. BMP stands for "bitmap," and refers to an image format where each pixel is represented by a single binary digit. These files are not compressed, and they provide a way to identify the color depth of an image. Some variations of BMP use different types of compression. The BMP file structure starts with a 14-byte header that describes the file, then the header DIB that provides further information about the bitmap and its pixel format, as illustrated in **Figure 9**.

The compressed version of BMP comes with some optional functions like the Extra Bitmasks. An optional color table is also included in this structure, which is followed by the Gap1 block that defines the alignment structure of the file. The Pixel array structure is mandatory and present in every BMP file, which specifies the value of each pixel. It varies in size. The next two structures, Gap2 and ICC color profiles, are optional and vary in size. They help manage the colors [35]. Our algorithm has shown that the BMP format produces the best results in terms of detectability and size increase after embedding. To demonstrate this, we conducted an experiment where we embedded a stego message of 4096 bytes into various file formats of the same image. The purpose of this experiment was to compare detectability while taking into consideration the size increase after embedding. The following text displays the outcome of this experiment.

The BMP file format has optional functions such as the Extra Bitmasks, which can be used with the compressed version of BMP. Additionally, a color table is included in this optional structure along with the color pixel array and the Gap1 block, which defines the alignment structure of the file. The pixel array structure is mandatory in every BMP file to determine the specific value of each pixel, and its size varies. The next two structures are optional. In this report, we present the results of an experiment where a stego message of 4.096 bytes was embedded into different file formats

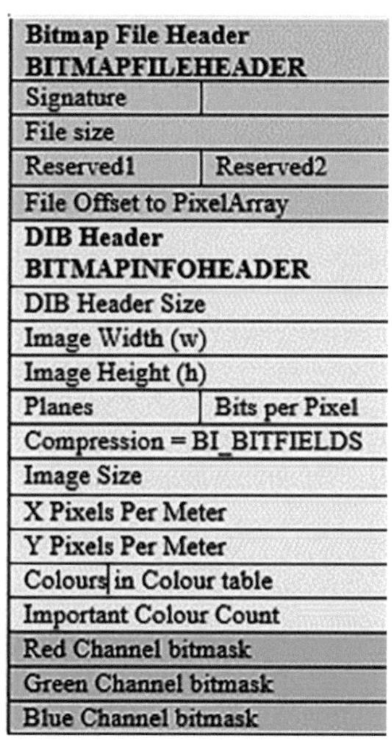

Figure 9.
A BMP file structure.

of the same image. The objective was to compare detectability while considering the size increase after embedding the message. We began by analyzing the exploitation of image formats and frequency domain techniques, providing a quick introduction to these topics. The simplest technique used for embedding data inside the file is exploiting areas where usually no data is kept. This technique does not alter the content of the file but is visible when looking at the source code and placeholder. BMP has shown the best results in several aspects.

The report discusses various methods of applied steganography, including simpler methods such as EOF and EXIF. However, the report focuses on a more advanced technique that combines Discrete Cosine Transform with well-known technologies to enhance steganography and improve copyright protection. Discrete Cosine functions were used as they are the best-known mathematical periodic functions. Fourier series were also employed to analyze a periodic function into its constituent components and send signals without distortion. The technique involves breaking images into sub-bands, deleting high-frequency components and using only real numbers for JPEG compression. **Figure 10** illustrates the standard DCT algorithm that contains LSB, as shown in **Figures 11** and **12**. When embedding, the images are broken into four

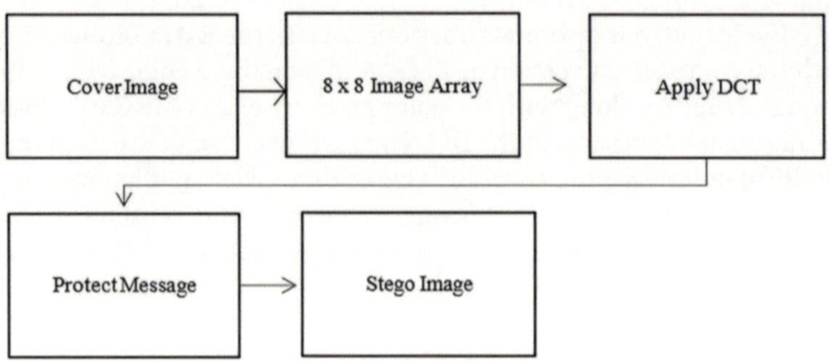

Figure 10.
A basic DCT algorithm.

Figure 11.
8 × 8 base matrix of DCT.

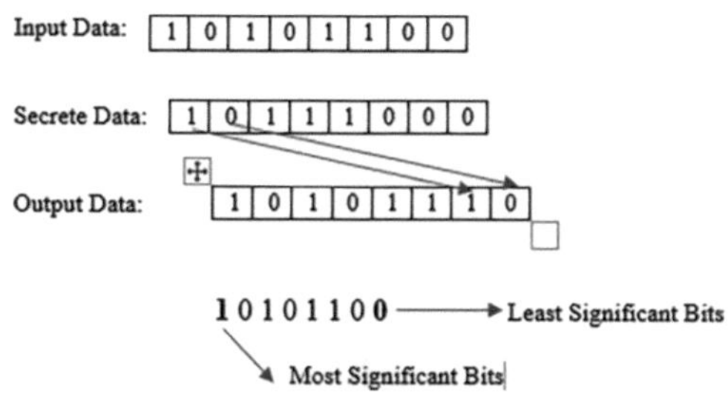

Figure 12.
LSB and MSB insertion example.

steps before applying DCT and genetic algorithms. The Cosine Transform algorithm code simulates breaking the figure into partitions of an 8x8 block, which is then reassembled.

Quantization is a signal processing technique that involves rounding and truncating a matrix setup. Matrix multiplication is then performed and the result is stored in a temporary matrix N × N.

This procedure involves using cosine to re-multiply and generate the final matrix. The value is then quantized and rounded to an integer. The inverse operation is the next step, which outputs 0 to 255 values for the pixels in an N*N matrix. **Figure 12** above illustrates the concept of Least Significant Bits (LSB) and Most Significant Bits (MSB) of an image array. DCT incorporates LSB as part of the technique, in addition to other measures it includes for confusion and diffusion. This adds more complexity to the distribution of secret data, strengthening the security of the algorithm beyond just using LSB alone. Every pixel has 24 bits, to modify a pixel programmatically would depend on the algorithm used, but it is easier to use a sequence. The pixels to be modified must be selected randomly, using pseudo-random, and the algorithm needs to remember which pixel is picked. Examples of algorithms' methods to change the file and embed content would include a region of the file to be replaced, for example, edges, highest frequency, and least significant bits. There is a choice to pick one bit in a byte or more. To minimize the number of modified pixels, we primarily employ the LSB algorithm (Least Significant Bits), and the number of altered bits per pixel is directly linked to the Data rate. When we use algorithms that try to concentrate all the confidential data in as few pixels as possible, we are more likely to get visual distortion and be more vulnerable to statistical analysis, as on the algorithms we simulated previously. Hence, modifying as few pixels as possible will make data contained in one place which will be discoverable easier and be more vulnerable to statistical analysis. Some of the key issues are illustrated in **Figure 12**.

The process of hiding data in an image involves compressing the image, which in turn leads to increased distortion as the image quality decreases. It is crucial to note that this method is sensitive to statistical analysis, and using specific bits to hide data can make it easily detectable. Some algorithms only output black or black-and-white images after data is hidden. Furthermore, the capacity to hide data is limited, as it can only hide data in specific bits of an image, such as LSB, HSB, and specific colors.

Detecting steganography can be done by observing distortion in the file. However, visible distortion is not always a reliable indicator. Mathematical algorithms can help identify hidden content, but some algorithms may have minimal distortion and still be detectable by statistical analysis. It's important to note that some images may be distorted due to resizing, and not because of steganography. For example, they are

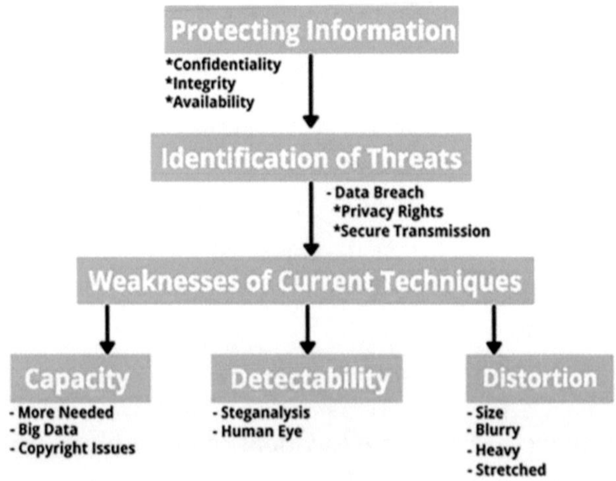

Figure 13.
Issues of DCT as a steganography technique.

stretching an image too much by maximizing or minimizing it. One algorithm that may not always show distortion is LSB. The content hidden by LSB is located in the least significant bits of the carrier file. Mathematical algorithms can be applied to identify the LSB capability.

Different algorithms have different capacities for measuring hidden content. The least significant bits are often the easiest targets for steganalysis. Other algorithms, such as those that search for specific colors, can also restrict capacity. **Figure 13** provides more examples. The Discrete Cosine Transform method algorithms are widely used in the Steganography Transform Domain, but there are still weaknesses that need improvement. The capacity, distortion, and detectability of DCT depend on the amount of data on the carrier file. The coefficient bits in the transform domain of the file are used to hide content in the stego-image.

For instance, let us consider an 8 x 8 block per RGB (Red, Green, and Blue). This converts into 64 coefficients that undergo DCT compression and quantisation. Additionally, LSB is used to substitute the image coefficients with the secret content. However, there is a need for more capacity with minimal distortion and detectability so that more data can be hidden securely. Creating a superior quality stego-image that can be measured by dB is the ultimate goal.

Therefore, we simulated and tested improvements for our new algorithm using distributed Steganography and a mix of methods that worked well to enhance Steganography itself. Our analysis of different digital data files helped us determine the best one to use for securing content while improving capacity and minimizing detectability and distortion.

3. Conclusion

The main weaknesses of current Big Data techniques have been identified, and important points for analysis and investigation have been highlighted. The DSoBMP-I approach can address the low capacity, high detectability, and distortion issues that are common in most steganographic algorithms used today, particularly DCT. After experimenting with different ideas and image formats, it was found that BMP is the best image type for embedding data. To ensure better flexibility, two useful encryption algorithms were demonstrated in case the embedded data or files are large and complex, and extra security is needed. Additionally, a new method of distributing personal data into a set of images was proposed, based on the original file supplied, along with the choice of partition size.

This approach has been shown to increase capacity by 100% when compared to other algorithms that do not consider file format as a crucial factor and do not have access to distributed Steganography. It achieves this by using a simple 2x2 matrix, and the capacity further increases as the matrix size increases. This approach has been proven to be more powerful than previous research, such as Nidhi's study mentioned in the text. The algorithm used in this research has proven to be superior to previous methods. The result of 68db of power achieved in this method surpasses the results of other research that highlighted the power of 30db in 2010 and 65db in 2015, with similar experiments. This is a significant step forward. The detectability and distortion are not easily noticeable, and hence, we recommend using the DSoBMP-I methodology proposed here for securing copyright materials and big data.

The improved security of the steganography algorithm is attributed to two factors: a larger spatial domain for embedding the secret data and the use of digital data files with cleaner pixels. By distributing the data across more files, we increase the area available for embedding, which in turn results in less distortion and less detectability due to random allocation. Furthermore, encryption in a larger domain using the most efficient techniques was tested during this research and compared with other approaches and files. Practitioners already using steganography today will benefit from extra security and less distortion and detectability of their copyright data on their images, they will also benefit from embedding more details on their copyright note, license terms, history of the file or metadata of the image, more data can be recorded and kept safe. In summary, improving capacity provided the largest set of significant clusters for this investigation or in other words having a bigger space to embed data, also improves the security of the secret message as it will be distributed in a bigger domain hence it will also have less detectability and distortion.

The uniqueness of the new algorithm and our published papers cited already by other researchers are proof of the contribution to knowledge. In this report, we have a clear guide of historical and current techniques in steganography, apart from highlighting where criminals can embed secret information on PDFs for investigators to analyze, the author identified the best file to use to embed data to secure copyrights and tackled weaknesses of Steganography with a new algorithm to enhance the security of the technique.

There is always room for improvement in any project, and this research is no different. With this research topic, the author was able to gain knowledge on how Steganography can be used in diverse ways and different technologies and how it still needs to grow to be able to survive big data and the cybercriminals that make use of it. It was remarkably interesting to know exactly where data can be hidden to follow up on further Steganalysis projects and Steganography itself, used for thousands of years, sometimes people might think that it could be dying, but it is not dying, it is growing stronger so that it might need to be better regulated in the future. Other researchers can start their work straight away after learning the best file to embed data from this research, the weaknesses of current techniques, how to address the issues and considerations for extra security for applications and improvements suggested here.

We aimed to protect copyright data and improve security, but improving security is an ongoing task as digital criminals are always inventing new ways of breaking algorithms to achieve their targets. The strongest part of the work is the good analysis and contents on several different methods shown here and using different data files to show and simulate steganography in various forms using different techniques, while the weakest part is attributed to the design of the prototype, the author wanted to create a web application to add copyright to images and ensure they all carry the data across the web to identify the owners and creators, but it is rather disappointing the number of obstacles behind the international medium Internet, how we regulate the Internet to make this happen is a question that needs to be answered before this is made possible for the public and with big data, snipping tools and other applications that can copy images.

The most interesting findings and recommendations are how data can be manipulated in different ways and embedded inside different files, masked, and compressed and how criminals even with the technology we have today can still distribute a virus over the internet without leaving any traces, the more technology evolves, the more cybercriminals evolve, and how difficult it is for us to have these "traces" and records from the origin of files, finding the real owners of the data over the web because the internet is not regulated well. The author has always been in favor of freedom of expression on the web, but after investigating steganography and eavesdropping, we need to think of ways of regulating and attributing ownership to files and information circulating on the internet. For the proposed further research, the author would start by concentrating on legal issues of the internet medium, researching on providing guidelines to regulate it better or part of it to be able to identify ways of making sure we can cope with Big Data in terms of attributing ownership to internet users and creative personnel, authors or creators, definitely embedding precise location from where images are created, then carrying logs of where and who has accessed specific materials from specific sites. This would be extremely challenging as the internet is an international medium regulated by different laws from different regions and because of the number of logs that had to be recorded by someone in an exceptionally large server which would be expensive, but for easier starts, this research can also progress by improving the design of the current solution.

Extra considerations with eavesdropping and snipping image tools, embedding data via the WIFI can also add security as data can leak while being embedded plus the research for the new smart data traveling the network with embedded characteristics from the owner is complex but still worth researching more. The improvements never stop, and we should consider protecting the data while embedding it on the network and limiting the clients that "purchase" the software.

In the next session of this chapter, we will encounter the references used to accomplish this research. Published work in international journals such as Springer includes experiments on PDF by highlighting exactly where steganography can be added to identify malicious intents, as well as security awareness for eavesdropping data from mobile devices and the improved algorithm to use steganography to tackle weaknesses of current techniques to secure copyright materials like images from smartphones of creators as an example, but from the process of doing a PhD, the author learnt, apart from the knowledge in this field, that there will not be a time when we have all the answers and we will know everything, technology is always changing, the more we read, the more we learn, and the more questions we have, and we can always research more and as we find fixes for a problem, another one arises, and we can always learn more. The advice the author would give to researchers entering this area is to follow the recommendations of this chapter for a straightforward start on your research and focus on one problem at a time, as in real life, the issues and work to strengthen security never ends.

Acknowledgements

A big thanks to my beloved mother Veronica Maria de Araujo who always persuaded me to complete my doctorate and kept me motivated to continue the research, never stop searching for answers and believing in Science. Another big thanks goes to my husband Adriano Ribeiro da Cruz for always being present in all hard and good moments throughout my academic life facilitating the completion of research work. In addition, my rescued dog Mickle Pickle, my black ex-racer greyhound provided joy and mental stability through the kindness in her eyes, smile and company for exercise walks during her retirement.

Author details

Istteffanny Isloure Araujo
Intelligent Systems Research Group, School of Computing and Digital Media, London Metropolitan University, London, UK

*Address all correspondence to: i.araujo@londonmet.ac.uk

References

[1] Kalaivanan SA. A survey on digital image steganography. International Journal of Emerging Trends and Technology in Computer Science. 2015;**17**:30-33

[2] Zhang R, Dong S, Liu J. Invisible steganography via generative adversarial networks. Multimedia Tools and Applications. 2018;**78**:8559-8575. DOI: 10.1007/s11042-018-6951-z

[3] Koptyra K, Ogiela M. Distributed steganography in PDF files—Secrets hidden in modified pages. Entropy. 2020;**22**(6):30-59

[4] Mills R. The Metadata in JPEG files. 2018. Available from: https://dev.exiv2.org/projects/exiv2/wiki/The_Metadata_in_JPEG_files [Accessed: May 15, 2021]

[5] Chandramoulia R, Memon N. Steganography Capacity: A Steganalysis Perspective. Vol. 1(1). New York, USA: A Department of E.C.E., Stevens Institute of Technology; 2015. pp. 1-5

[6] Kawaguchi E. Applications of Steganography. 2015. Available from: http://datahide.org/BPCSe/applications-e.html

[7] Jahankhani H et al. Conference proceedings. In: Jahankhani H et al., editors. Global E-Security. London: Springer; 2011. pp. 23-25

[8] Siper A et al. The rise of steganography. Proceedings of Student/Faculty Research Day. 2005;**1**(1):1

[9] Korus P, Białas J, Dziech A. Multimedia Tools and Applications. 2014;**68**:59. DOI: 10.1007/s11042-011-0986-8

[10] Mondal B, Mandat T. A Secret Shearing Algorithm based on LSB Substitution. 2014. Available from: https://www.researchgate.net/figure/A-typical-diagram-of-LSB-Substitution-techniques_fig1_262996420 [Accessed: May 15, 2021]

[11] Borse D, Patil S. Review on transform domain steganographic techniques (DCT and DWT). International Journal of Innovative Research in Computer and Communication Engineering. 2015;**3**(12):12466-12473

[12] Thampi SM. Information hiding techniques: A tutorial review. LBS College of Engineering. 2007;**1**:1-15

[13] Dave HP. Steganography technique based on DCT coefficients. International Journal of Engineering Research and Applications. 2012;**2**:713-717

[14] Elham Ghasemi JS. High-capacity image steganography using wavelet transform and genetic algorithm. Proceeding of the International Multiconference of Engineers and Computer Scientists. 2011;**1**:495-498

[15] Manda N. Image authentication technique in frequency domain based on discrete Fourier. Proceedings of ICCS. 2010;**125**:144-147

[16] Mazurczyk W, Karaś M, Szczypiorski K, et al. YouSkyde: Information hiding for skype video traffic. Multimedia Tools and Applications. 2016;**75**:13521

[17] Rana S, Sur A. View invariant DIBR-3D image watermarking using DT-CWT. Multimedia Tools and Applications. 2018;**79**:1-29. DOI: 10.1007/s11042-018-7024-z

[18] Tataru R et al. Is hidden data safe? Analysis of the public

cryptand hide-steganos application. Proceedings of the Romanian Academy. 2015;**16**(1):299-312

[19] Leiner B, et al. Brief History of the Internet. 2017. Available from: http://www.internetsociety.org/internet/what-internet/history-internet/brief-history-internet

[20] Zielińska E et al. Development trends in steganography. Institute of Telecommunications. 2015;**1**(1):1-13

[21] Antony N. Improved capacity collage steganography using discrete cosine transformation. International Journal of Scientific and Engineering Research. 2015;**6**(11):1060-1064

[22] Cameron L. With Cryptography Easier to Detect, Cybercriminals Now Hide Malware in Plain Sight. Call It Steganography. Here's How It Works. 2018. Available from: https://publications.computer.org/computer-magazine/2018/11/15/how-steganography-works/ [Accessed: May 16, 2021]

[23] Evsutin O, Melman A, Meshcheryakov O. Digital steganography and watermarking for digital images: A review of current research directions. IEEE. 2020;**8**(1):166589-166611

[24] Al-Thahab O, Hussein A. Implementation of stego-watermarking technique by encryption image based on turbo code for copyright application. IEEE. 2020;**1**(1):148-153

[25] Garg M, Gupta S, Khatri P. Fingerprint watermarking and steganography for ATM transactions using LSB-RSA and 3-DWT algorithm. IEEE. 2015;**48**(1):246-251

[26] Checkpoint. Infosec 2015 - Data Center Security. Infosec 2015- Data Center Security, Check Point. London: Tele Group Ltd.; 2015

[27] Sanyal T. Reversible and Irreversible Data Hiding Technique. Hyderabad, India: Neudesic India Pvt. Limited; 2014. pp. 1-4

[28] Barlow J. Chapter 20. In: Barlow J, editor. Copyright and Privacy Protection. Cambridge: University of Cambridge; 2014. pp. 424-452

[29] Neil Johnson Z. Information Hiding: Steganography and Watermarking-Attacks and Countermeasures. New York: Springer Science + Business; 2012

[30] Shankdhar P. Best Tools to Perform Steganography. Wisconsin, USA: Infosec Institute; 2015. pp. 1-10

[31] Bhure SB. Data encryption by image steganography. International Journal of Information and Computation Technology. 2014;**4**:453-458

[32] Sadhana G. Strengthening the security of information use. International Journal of Computer Science and Information Technology Research. 2014;**2**:27-35

[33] Poretsky S. How to decrypt messages embedded within images. CHron. 2016;**143**:1-5

[34] Kalaivanan SA. A survey on digital image steganography. International Journal of Emerging Trends and Technology in Computer Science. 2016;**1**:30-33

[35] Ramapriya B. An improved approach of text steganography in application with rotational symmetry. International Journal of Innovative Research in Computer and Communication Engineering. 2017;**5**(7):12939-12947

Chapter 2

Recent Advances in Steganography

Mahmud Ahmad Bamanga, Aliyu Kamalu Babando and Mohammed Ahmed Shehu

Abstract

This chapter explores the diverse uses of steganography, a complex technique of hiding messages within everyday objects, across several sectors. The chapter focuses on the applications of steganography in finance and banking, healthcare, medical data security, and intellectual property. It examines the reasons, methods, advantages, and difficulties involved in adopting steganography. Furthermore, it elucidates the prospective trajectories and ramifications of this clandestine means of communication. The study also examines the function of steganography in organisational communication, highlighting its capacity to bolster security, facilitate hidden communication, and guarantee adherence to rules. The chapter ends with a thorough examination of the issues related to privacy, ethics, laws, and regulations that are associated with steganography. Lastly, it visualises the future path of this influential technology, highlighting the significance of openness, public knowledge, and cooperation for conscientious and moral advancement.

Keywords: security, privacy, compressed media, covert communication, data integrity and steganalysis

1. Introduction

Steganography is a complex technique that includes hiding information within seemingly harmless carriers to enable secret communication [1]. It comes from the Greek words "steganos" (covered) and "graphia" (writing). Within the realm of digital technology, this clandestine communication tactic involves concealing confidential information within various forms of media, such as pictures, sound, or videos, with the main objective of avoiding detection by unintended individuals. The basic framework of steganography is based on the core idea of hiding information in a way that it is not easily detectable, thereby assuring the concealed payload remains undetectable [2]. Steganography, a unique field with several applications such as cybersecurity, digital forensics, and secure communication, deviates from traditional cryptography by emphasising the encryption of message contents.

Steganography is the practice of hiding messages within ordinary media, and it has fascinated people for its capacity to conceal information in a way that is not obvious. In contrast to cryptography, which obfuscates the actual content of a message, steganography is concerned with concealing the mere presence of the communication [3]. The purpose of this covert technique is to conceal confidential data within a "cover object," which is usually a picture, audio file, a written document, or network protocol. The objective is to make the hidden information undetectable to the human eye, standard analysis tools, and even advanced steganalysis algorithms [4].

According to [5], there are three key concepts that form the basis of this concealing.

i. Embedding Capacity refers to the maximum quantity of confidential information that can be concealed within the cover object without affecting its perceived quality or arousing suspicion.

ii. Imperceptibility refers to the extent to which the alteration made to the object in order to conceal the data is indistinguishable from its original form.

iii. Robustness refers to the capacity of concealed information to endure alterations or distortions that may occur while the cover object is transmitted or stored.

2. A brief overview of steganographic techniques

A review of steganographic techniques discloses a wide range of ways used to insert and hide information into digital carriers. Historically, conventional methods of steganography, as described in [6], entailed modifying the least significant bits of binary data in images, audio, or video files in order to conceal confidential information.

There are various methods available to accomplish steganographic objectives, which can be classified into four general groups. These strategies collectively contribute to the complex terrain of steganography, always adapting to answer the challenges faced by developments in detection technologies:

The technique known as Least Significant Bit (LSB) insertion involves altering the least significant bits of data values in the cover object to encode the secret message [7]. The simplicity of [4] allows for easy access, but its capacity for embedding is restricted and it is highly vulnerable to steganalysis.

Spatial Domain Techniques (SDT); these methods utilise the redundancy or noise-like regions present in the cover object to incorporate information. Illustrative instances involve altering the amounts of brightness in pixels inside images [8] or manipulating the carrier frequencies in music [3].

Transform Domain Techniques (TDT) use the use of mathematical transformations, such as the Discrete Cosine Transform (DCT), to embed data into the modified coefficients of the cover object [9]. These strategies frequently provide enhanced embedding capacity and imperceptibility as compared to spatial domain methods.

Cover Selection and Generation (CS&G) refers to the process of selecting or creating cover objects that possess statistical features ideal for effectively concealing information. This can be achieved by either choosing cover objects having inherent properties that make them good for hiding information, as discussed in [10], or by producing synthetic cover objects that are particularly designed for steganography, as mentioned in [11]. The use of CS&G techniques can significantly enhance the concealment of hidden information.

3. A journey through steganography's past and present

Exploring the history and complexity of steganography reveals a fascinating progression from the past to the present. Steganography, an ancient art of encrypting information for secure transmission, has smoothly migrated into the digital era [8]. In the early digital era, a technique called Least Significant Bit (LSB) replacement was commonly used in image-based steganography. This method involves modifying the least significant bits of binary data.

With the shift towards multimedia, there was a development of image-based approaches. The utilisation of frequency domain transformations, such as the discrete cosine transform (DCT) mentioned in Ref. [9], and the discrete wavelet transform (DWT) mentioned in Ref. [2], offered more advanced techniques for incorporating information while preserving perceptual quality. Starting from [12], audio and video files emerged as new areas of exploration, where spread spectrum techniques were employed to distribute concealed data throughout the carrier signal in order to reduce the chances of detection. Mathematical transformations were utilised in audio steganography to seamlessly insert information, particularly in the transform domain [8].

The exploration of steganography also involves the ongoing difficulties presented by detection. The collaboration between steganographers and cybersecurity professionals has resulted in the creation of sophisticated algorithms for identifying hidden communication [1]. In order to uncover hidden data, it is necessary to constantly improve digital forensics tools in response to the ever-changing landscape [13]. Steganography has adopted state-of-the-art technologies in the contemporary period. The combination of machine learning and deep learning algorithms brings about a significant change, introducing unparalleled complexity in the hiding of information inside digital media [14]. The progression mentioned in [1] not only improves the security of concealed communication, but also presents new difficulties for cybersecurity professionals who are working to identify progressively more subtle modifications.

Steganography has a long history, dating back thousands of years. The ancient Greeks used invisible ink and tablets wrapped in wax to hide communications [15]. Over the course of history, methods have advanced in conjunction with technology, progressing from concealing microdots within images during World War II [16] to capitalising on data redundancies in digital media during the internet age. The advent of the digital revolution has significantly accelerated the progress of steganographic innovations. The extensive data storage capability of digital media, combined with advancements in processing power, has facilitated the creation of advanced embedding algorithms and cover selection procedures. Notable advancements comprise:

Deep learning-based embedding involves the use of neural networks to hide information within complex media such as photos and movies. This technique allows for a higher capacity of information to be hidden while maintaining imperceptibility [17]. Homomorphic encryption enables performing computations on encrypted data, hence facilitating secure steganographic processes without the need for decryption [18]. Covert channels in AI systems involve utilising the intrinsic properties of AI models to hide information that can only be deciphered by trained models, hence providing an innovative level of security [19].

These innovations broaden the scope of steganography, surpassing its conventional uses such as clandestine communication and copyright safeguarding. Businesses are currently investigating the possibilities of utilising blockchain technology for safe data exchange [20], supply chain traceability, digital rights management, and even improving user privacy in communication systems [21].

The evolution of steganography from ancient methods of hiding information to its complex techniques in modern times demonstrates its ability to withstand and adjust to different historical periods. Examining its historical and current aspects emphasises its ongoing importance in guaranteeing safe communication in a constantly changing digital environment.

4. Steganography workflow

The steganography workflow, as depicted in **Figure 1**, is the elaborate procedure of hiding confidential data within a different digital file, known as a carrier file. This can have multiple objectives, including ensuring secure connection, concealing data storage, or even facilitating artistic expression.

Figure 1 illustrates the procedure of encrypting and concealing confidential data within a carrier file to provide secure transmission or storage in a corporate setting. As outlined below:

i. *Identify Sensitive Information:* The initial stage entails identifying the secret data that requires safeguarding. Such information may encompass bank records, commercial secrets, personal particulars, or other vital data.

ii. *Choose Carrier File:* Then, you choose an appropriate carrier file to incorporate the confidential information. The carrier file can encompass a range of digital formats, including photos, documents, audio, and video files. To ensure that the hidden data goes unnoticed, it is crucial to select a file that has sufficient capacity to handle it.

iii. *Steganographic Techniques (Encode):* This step entails utilising steganographic techniques to encode the confidential information into the selected carrier

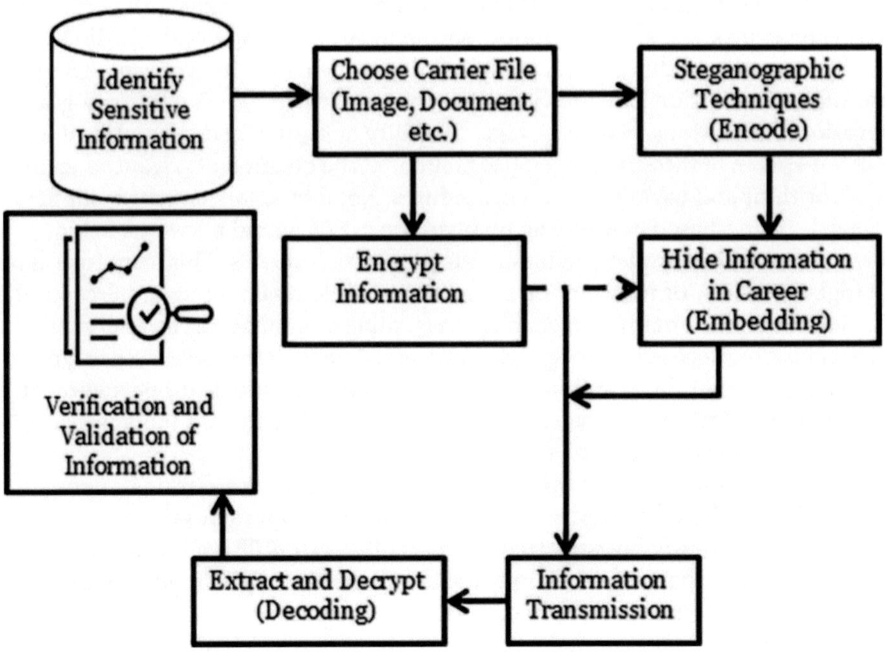

Figure 1.
The steganography workflow.

file. Various methodologies are available, each possessing distinct merits and drawbacks. Several conventional techniques include: Least Significant Bit (LSB), Spread Spectrum and Parity Embedding.

iv. *Encrypt Information (Optional):* Enhanced security can be attained by encrypting the confidential data prior to incorporating it into the carrier file. This encryption process provides an additional layer of security in the event that the steganography is somehow breached.

v. *Hide Information in Carrier (Embedding):* The encoded data is concealed within the selected carrier file using the chosen steganographic method. The objective is to modify the carrier file with minimal changes in order to evade detection.

vi. *Extract and Decrypt Information (Decoding):* At the receiving end, the concealed information must be retrieved from the carrier file. The encoded data is recovered by applying the inverse of the embedding procedure.

vii. *Information Transmission:* After extraction, the information may potentially be decrypted if it had been previously encrypted. At last, the obtained confidential data is now accessible for its intended purpose.

viii. *Verification and Validation of Information:* Following the process of embedding, it is of utmost importance to ensure that the information has been concealed accurately and can be effectively retrieved. This validation verifies that the steganographic procedure operated according to its intended purpose.

5. Balancing opportunities and challenges of steganography

Given the continuing growth of steganography, it is of utmost importance to carefully examine its impact on cybersecurity, privacy, and ethical considerations. The challenges of weighing the advantages of secure communication against the risks of misuse, such as cyberattacks or unlawful information transmission, and guaranteeing its responsible development are important issues that require continuous attention and discussion [22]. Various endeavours are currently in progress to tackle these challenges, which encompass:

i. *Development of robust steganalysis tools:* Enhancing the capacity to identify and extract concealed data is essential for reducing the risk of potential misuse [23].

ii. *Standardisation and Regulation:* It is crucial to create legal frameworks and ethical criteria to ensure responsible development and use of steganography [23].

iii. *Dissemination of information and instruction to the general public:* Enhancing public comprehension of the potential and constraints of steganography can contribute to its responsible application [22].

The future of steganography in [5] holds the potential for both exhilaration and intricacy. The potential of the sector to significantly improve secure communication, data protection, and user privacy is tremendous. Nonetheless, properly addressing the ethical and security concerns necessitates collaborative endeavours from researchers, developers, politicians, and consumers. To maintain the effectiveness of steganography as a means of communication and protection in the changing digital environment, it is important to encourage open discussions, adopt responsible development methods, and promote ongoing innovation [24].

6. Significance of steganography in contemporary business

In addition to transforming commerce, the digital era has unveiled a multitude of security concerns. Safeguarding sensitive data has become crucial as it infiltrates all facets of corporate activities, encompassing financial transactions and intellectual property. Allow us to acquaint you with steganography, a hitherto clandestine method of hiding messages from sight that is now emerging as a powerful asset in the arsenal of modern business.

Steganography provides enterprises with an extra level of security that surpasses conventional encryption methods, as it may discreetly embed sensitive data within seemingly harmless media files [22]. This capability surpasses the scope of covert espionage activities [25]. Steganography enhances concealment in a highly vulnerable digital landscape plagued by advanced assaults and data breaches, where conventional encryption is prone to decryption by persistent adversaries [22]. Businesses have the ability to transform regular files, such as photos, videos, audio recordings, and text documents, into secure communication channels. This is achieved by encoding hidden messages within the files themselves, making them resistant to both casual observation and advanced scanning systems [26]. This groundbreaking phenomenon has extensive impacts across various industries:

i. *Improved Cybersecurity:* Imagine commonplace email attachments or video conference recordings that contain confidential contracts, financial information, or strategic plans. Steganography ensures that data remains hidden and resistant to prolonged hacking attempts, so adding an extra level of protection against unauthorised access [27].

ii. *Ensuring the Security of Confidential Transactions:* Banks employ steganography to cryptographically secure confidential information, such as account numbers and payment amounts, by concealing them within apparently insignificant documents that accompany financial transactions [28].

iii. *Safeguarding Intellectual Property:* To ensure the protection of valuable intellectual property and avoid unauthorised acquisition of trade secrets, it is possible to discreetly incorporate exclusive designs, research discoveries, and marketing strategies into product photographs, presentations, or even staff training materials [26].

iv. *Ensuring Supply Chain Transparency:* Employing steganography to conceal production timestamps, distinct identifiers, and product origins within packaging or associated documents establishes an unalterable path that diminishes counterfeiting and enhances the ability to track products. This cultivates trust among consumers and regulatory bodies [29].

These examples merely touch upon the vast potential of steganography in the corporate realm [30]. The applications are expected to expand further as ongoing research and development yield more sophisticated and dependable techniques, thereby revolutionising security, data protection, and communication standards across various industries [31]. It is crucial to acknowledge the ethical difficulties and potential for misuse that are connected to this powerful tool, as indicated in [32]. To ensure that steganography is a beneficial tool for organisations to protect their important data assets and effectively traverse the digital landscape with a competitive advantage, responsible development, informed usage, and well-established regulatory frameworks are crucial [33].

The advent of steganography signifies a profound shift in the approach that corporations might choose for managing communication and ensuring data security. Due to its ability to hide sensitive and crucial information behind the guise of innocence, it has a significant impact on the modern business landscape [2, 3]. Steganography has the capacity to revolutionise the business environment and foster a digital realm that is characterised by increased transparency, security, and innovation, as ethical standards become more prevalent and technology advances.

6.1 The role of steganography in business

The risks to corporate data are always changing in tandem with the digital ecosystem. While traditional encryption techniques are essential, they may be insufficient in the face of prevalent cyberattacks and advanced breaches. Steganography, the process of concealing messages within seemingly harmless things, is a highly valuable instrument in today's corporate arsenal [34].

Steganography is the process of concealing information within a seemingly harmless digital medium, such as an image, video, or audio file. This is different from encryption, which transforms data into an incomprehensible format [25, 35, 36]. By rendering the data imperceptible to both advanced scanning systems and casual examination, the method of concealing it in plain sight, as described in [35], significantly diminishes the likelihood of detection. Due to this distinctive attribute, steganography can be employed to enhance data security procedures and enhance communication confidentiality in several commercial scenarios;

i. *Advocating for Secure Pathways for Communication:* Envision transmitting financial data, business strategies, or confidential contracts by discreetly integrating them into ordinary video conference records or related papers, instead than using encrypted emails. Steganography enables covert communication, enabling companies to exchange confidential information in risky environments without arousing suspicion. By utilising this feature, it becomes feasible to collaborate securely with associates, effectively safeguards against eavesdropping during international communication, and ensures the protection of confidential data from internal breaches [37].

ii. *Safeguarding Sensitive Data Assets:* Steganography provides a protective layer that goes beyond communication to ensure the security of important data assets utilised in company operations. Envision discreetly incorporating financial transaction information into unrelated supplementary documents, embedding patient medical records into non-medical files, or placing product identifier codes within product images. This inconspicuous security measure minimises the likelihood of data breaches, thwarts unauthorised entry, and ensures the integrity of confidential information from inception to completion [2, 34].

iii. *Improving the Visibility and Clarity of the Supply Chain:* The presence of product tampering and counterfeit goods poses significant challenges in the interconnected supply chains of the modern globalised world. Steganography offers a solution by allowing the inclusion of manufacture timestamps, unique IDs, and product provenance within packaging or supporting documents. By establishing a tamper-proof trail, this enhances product traceability, cultivates customer trust, and protects the business's reputation [29].

iv. *The Complex Topography:* Ethical Dimensions and Deliberations Despite the numerous benefits of steganography, it is crucial to acknowledge its potential limitations and ethical considerations. To ensure responsible and sensible use of this powerful tool, its development is crucial. In order to prevent malicious exploitation and uphold ethical communication practices, it is crucial to establish well-defined regulatory frameworks and carry out awareness campaigns [38].

Steganography is a powerful and influential factor that is changing the way secure communication and data security are handled in the digital age, rather than being seen as a relic of the past [22]. Steganography, in the range of [1–3, 22], grants businesses a competitive advantage by offering an extra level of safeguarding that goes beyond standard encryption. This allows for secure communication routes and the protection of sensitive data. In a progressively data-sensitive setting, these organisations can operate with enhanced assurance. The potential of steganography in the business world will continue to expand as responsible practices and technical breakthroughs become more prevalent, hence enabling a more innovative, transparent, and secure future [4].

7. Brief overview of key applications and use cases of steganography

Steganography, due to its capacity to hide information within apparently harmless carriers, has been widely utilised in different fields [39]. The adaptability of this clandestine communication technique is shown in its primary applications and instances of use:

i. *Financial Transactions and Banking:* Steganography is crucial in ensuring the security of financial transactions and banking processes. By incorporating confidential data into digital carriers, it guarantees the privacy of financial information during transactions, reducing the possibility of interception or unauthorised access [28].

ii. *Intellectual Property Protection:* Digital watermarking, a technique of concealing information within digital media, is utilised to safeguard intellectual property. This tool provides robust protection for digital assets, including photographs, movies, and documents. It guarantees the integrity and authenticity of creative works, while effectively discouraging any unauthorised use or distribution [40].

iii. *Secure Communication within Organisations:* Steganography enables the establishment of secure communication channels among authorised workers in organisational contexts. This use case guarantees the covert transmission of sensitive information, hence improving the confidentiality of internal conversations and safeguarding proprietary corporate data [26].

iv. *Digital Marketing and Advertising:* Steganography is utilised in digital marketing and advertising to conceal information within multimedia content. By ensuring the integrity of adverts and preventing unauthorised adjustments, this contributes to the credibility of digital marketing [20].

v. *Military and Defence Communications:* Steganography is used in military and defence settings to ensure secure communication and discreetly send vital information. This use is especially useful in cases where maintaining anonymity is of utmost importance, and conventional encryption methods may not be adequate [21].

vi. *Journalism and Whistleblower Protection:* Steganography functions as a means for journalists and whistleblowers to safely send sensitive material. Through the act of embedding information into digital media, individuals can effectively transmit important data while reducing the likelihood of being detected, thus enabling the exposure of misconduct without jeopardising their anonymity [35].

vii. *Cybersecurity and Digital Forensics:* Steganography poses both difficulties and opportunities in the realm of cybersecurity and digital forensics. Although hackers may utilise steganalysis to conceal dangerous code or extract data, digital forensics experts employ steganalysis to identify concealed information and reveal possible security risks [27].

viii. *Scholarly Inquiry and Higher Education:* Steganography is utilised in research to carry out trials and investigations pertaining to the concealment of information. This encompasses the investigation of novel methodologies, the creation of defensive measures, and the progression of knowledge regarding the fundamental principles of clandestine communication [41].

The various applications presented in [42] demonstrate the versatility of steganography in effectively dealing with a broad range of modern difficulties. With the continuous advancement of technology, steganography is expected to have a greater impact, improving security and privacy in different areas.

8. Industry-specific applications of steganography

Beyond finance and banking, steganography is applied in a wide range of industries, each with its own distinct reasons and obstacles.

8.1 Steganography in finance and banking

Information is vital in the realm of finance. Each instance of clicking, swiping, and typing produces data that fuels the intricate algorithms propelling its system. In this expansive digital landscape, confidential data is continuously in motion, susceptible to surveillance and bad motives. However, in the midst of the commotion and openness, there is a clandestine kind of art that flourishes: steganography, the act of hiding messages in plain view [43].

This section explores the use of steganographic techniques in the finance and banking industry. We will analyse the reasons for using these covert tactics, reveal the precise techniques employed, and assess the inherent difficulties and possible weaknesses.

8.2 Motivations for financial steganography

Numerous variables contribute to the adoption of steganography in the financial industry:

i. *Improved Security:* Confidential financial information, such as account details, transaction data, and proprietary knowledge, can be concealed behind harmless cover sources such as photographs, papers, or audio files. This provides an additional level of security beyond traditional encryption, particularly when transmitted via public networks [21].

ii. *Regulatory Compliance:* Some financial regulations mandate the use of secure communication channels for particular categories of data. By integrating strong encryption, steganography can assist organisations in adhering to these requirements while maintaining efficiency and transparency [36].

iii. *Competitive Advantage:* Steganography can be used to hide market-sensitive information such as impending mergers, acquisitions, or investment strategies. This helps organisations gain a competitive edge by eliminating early leaks and insider trading [37].

iv. *Fraud Prevention:* Embedding covert watermarks or identity markers within financial papers and digital assets can enhance fraud detection and deter counterfeiting [38].

8.3 Techniques of financial steganography

A wide range of steganographic techniques is used in the financial domain:

i. *Text-based Techniques:* Information can be hidden within apparently ordinary documents such as reports, financial statements, or even emails. To encode binary representations of the concealed message, one can manipulate line spacing, font attributes, or punctuation [23, 41].

ii. *Image and Audio Steganography:* Financial data can be concealed within digital photos or audio files by altering attributes such as pixel colour values or audio frequencies [12]. Commonly employed techniques, such as least significant bit (LSB) modification and spread spectrum, are frequently utilised [7].

iii. *Network Traffic Steganography:* Concealed data can be encoded in the structure or timing of network packets transmitted across financial networks [44]. This enables clandestine communication between reliable nodes without arousing suspicion.

iv. *Blockchain-based Steganography:* Blockchain-based steganography is a topic of emerging study that investigates the use of blockchain technology as a hiding mechanism for steganographic techniques. This utilises the inherent security and unchangeability of blockchain networks to improve data secrecy [45].

8.4 Challenges and vulnerabilities of steganography

Although steganography in banking presents distinct benefits, it is not without of obstacles, which we outline as follows [4–6, 8, 39]:

i. *Detection and Steganalysis:* Advanced steganalysis technologies can be utilised to reveal concealed signals, particularly when the mechanism used for embedding is feeble or easily anticipated.

ii. *Limitations of Cover Source Capacity:* Steganography is sometimes constrained by the limited capacity of the cover source, which might hinder its usefulness for bigger data collections.

iii. *Legal and Ethical Considerations:* The utilisation of steganography in finance may give rise to legal and ethical considerations pertaining to data privacy, insider trading, or market manipulation, contingent upon the context and content of the concealed information.

iv. *Technological Dependency:* Steganographic approaches are reliant on particular software and algorithms. Flaws in these tools have the potential to jeopardise the security of concealed data.

8.5 Future directions and implications of steganography

The future of steganography in banking holds great potential and offers intriguing opportunities [19, 32, 36]:

i. *Incorporation of Artificial Intelligence:* Utilising machine learning algorithms can enhance the effectiveness and adaptability of steganographic approaches, hence increasing the capacity for data concealment and improving resistance to steganalysis.

ii. *Quantum Steganography:* The emerging area of quantum information theory presents intriguing possibilities for highly secure steganographic techniques that can withstand even the most advanced attacks.

iii. *Standardisation and Regulation:* With the increasing prevalence of steganography, there may be a need for industry-wide norms and regulations to ensure responsible and ethical use specifically within the financial sector.

9. Role of steganography in healthcare and medical data security

Healthcare facilities in the digital era produce and retain substantial quantities of delicate medical data, including patient records, imaging scans, and genetic information. Consequently, they become highly attractive targets for cyberattacks and data breaches [46]. Safeguarding this sensitive information is of utmost importance in order to preserve patient confidentiality, guarantee precise diagnoses, and uphold ethical principles. Although standard encryption is important for data security, steganography, the practice of hiding signals within ordinary items, is becoming a valuable tool in healthcare security [37].

9.1 Motivations for steganography in healthcare

Various factors contribute to the widespread use of steganography in the healthcare sector [46–48]:

i. *Improved Privacy:* By including medical data into seemingly harmless media formats such as photos, audio files, or medical scans, an additional level of security is achieved that surpasses traditional encryption methods, particularly when transmitted over public networks.

ii. *Adherence to Regulations:* Stringent regulations such as HIPAA and GDPR require the implementation of strong data security procedures. By integrating steganography with encryption, healthcare practitioners may adhere to these standards while ensuring the integrity of the data remains intact.

iii. *Anonymization and De-identification:* Confidential patient information such as names, addresses, and diagnoses can be hidden within medical photographs or reports using steganography. This allows for study and collaboration while ensuring the privacy of patients.

iv. *Telemedicine and Remote Consultations:* Steganography can be employed to securely communicate confidential medical information, such as diagnosis reports or patient scans, during remote consultations, so maintaining confidentiality and privacy.

9.2 Techniques employed for adopting steganography in healthcare

Different steganographic methods are used in the healthcare field [12, 48, 49]:

i. *Image and Audio Steganography:* Medical images such as X-rays or audio recordings of consultations can be employed to conceal patient data or diagnostic information by utilising methods like least significant bit (LSB) alteration or spread spectrum.

ii. *Text-based Steganography:* Patient information can be hidden within apparently innocuous clinical reports, medical notes, or research papers by modifying formatting, punctuation, or spacing in a manner that does not impact legibility.

iii. *Medical Signal Steganography:* Electrocardiogram (ECG) or electroencephalogram (EEG) recordings can be utilised as cover sources to conceal supplementary medical data or patient identities.

iv. *Blockchain-based Steganography:* Ongoing research investigates the use of blockchain technology as a hiding mechanism for steganographic methods, taking use of its inherent security and unchangeability to improve data concealment.

DOI: http://dx.doi.org/10.5772/intechopen.1004521

9.3 Benefits and challenges of steganography in healthcare

Although steganography in healthcare shows potential, it also presents a distinct set of obstacles [48–50]:

i. *Computer Overhead:* The process of embedding and extracting data might require a significant amount of computer resources, which may have an impact on the efficiency of workflow, particularly when dealing with huge datasets.

ii. *Steganalysis Vulnerability:* Advanced steganalysis methods have the potential to detect concealed data, particularly if the method used for embedding is feeble or easily anticipated.

iii. *Ethical Considerations:* The act of incorporating patient data, even if it is made anonymous, into other forms of media gives rise to ethical concerns that necessitate thorough examination and obtaining informed consent.

iv. *Regulatory Uncertainty:* The current legal and regulatory framework of steganography in healthcare is still developing, necessitating cautious manoeuvring to ensure adherence to the rules.

9.4 Future direction and implications of steganography in healthcare

The potential of steganography in healthcare is promising and offers intriguing prospects [48, 51]:

i. *Integration with AI and Machine Learning:* The utilisation of machine learning algorithms can enhance the effectiveness of steganographic techniques by increasing their capacity to hide data and making them more resistant to steganalysis.

ii. *Quantum Steganography:* The emerging domain of quantum information theory presents intriguing possibilities for highly secure steganographic techniques, offering enhanced data safeguarding.

iii. *Standardisation and Regulation:* With the increasing use of steganography, there may arise a need for industry-wide standards and rules to ensure responsible and ethical use in the healthcare field.

10. Applications of steganography in intellectual property

Intellectual property (IP) is of great significance in today's information-centric society, as it has substantial value for individuals, corporations, and institutions [40]. Ensuring the security of this intangible property from unauthorised use, duplication, or infringement is essential for promoting innovation and guaranteeing fair competition. Although classic approaches such as watermarking and encryption are important, steganography, which involves hiding messages within ordinary things, is becoming a new and innovative tool for protecting intellectual property.

10.1 Why steganography for IP protection?

There are numerous causes that contribute to the increasing interest in steganography for the purpose of protecting intellectual property:

i. *Enhanced Security:* Steganography provides an additional level of protection that surpasses traditional techniques such as watermarks, hence increasing the difficulty for unauthorised personnel to identify and eliminate concealed information [21].

ii. *Covert Authentication:* Concealing identifiable markers or watermarks within digital assets such as papers, photographs, or software enables unobtrusive confirmation of ownership and genuineness, hence assisting in the prevention of counterfeiting [27].

iii. *Resilience against Piracy:* Steganography can enhance resilience against piracy by embedding copyright data or digital licences directly into the content, making unauthorised copying and distribution more difficult or deterred [31].

iv. *Proof of Ownership:* Embedding distinct and chronologically recorded data into digital assets provides undeniable evidence of ownership, hence potentially bolstering legal assertions in the event of infringement [52].

10.2 Techniques employed in adopting steganography for IP protection

Numerous steganographic methods are utilised for intellectual property (IP) protection [21, 27, 52]:

i. *Text-based Techniques:* Ownership information or access codes can be incorporated into text documents such as patents, design specifications, or source code by changing punctuation, character spacing, or font attributes.

ii. *Image and Audio Steganography:* Images linked to patents, product designs, or copyrighted works can be utilised to hide ownership data or watermarks by employing methods such as least significant bit (LSB) alteration or spread spectrum.

iii. *Multimedia Steganography:* Video files or 3D models can serve as cover sources to conceal ownership information or authentication data, providing further security for intricate digital assets.

iv. *Network Traffic Steganography:* Network traffic steganography involves concealing ownership data or digital licences within the metadata or structure of network packets that are used to transfer digital assets. This technique can provide added protection throughout the online dissemination of these goods.

10.3 Benefits and challenges of steganography for IP protection

Though steganography shows potential in safeguarding intellectual property, it also presents a distinct set of difficulties [48, 51, 52]:

i. *Computer Overhead:* The process of embedding and extracting data may require significant computer resources, which can have a negative influence on workflow efficiency, particularly when dealing with huge datasets.

ii. *Steganalysis Vulnerability:* Advanced steganalysis tools have the potential to detect concealed information, particularly if the method used for embedding is feeble or easily anticipated.

iii. *Legal and Ethical Concerns:* The utilisation of steganography in intellectual property protection raises important legal and ethical issues. It is crucial to carefully assess the ramifications, assuring adherence to copyright laws and preventing any misuse for deceptive reasons.

iv. *Standardisation and Regulation:* The absence of uniform steganographic techniques and explicit laws can pose difficulties in legally enforcing and preventing potential misuse.

10.4 Future direction and implications of steganography for IP protection

The potential for steganography in safeguarding intellectual property (IP) is highly promising [27, 51, 52]:

i. *Incorporation of AI and Machine Learning:* The utilisation of machine learning algorithms can enhance the effectiveness and adaptability of steganographic approaches, hence increasing the capacity for data concealment and fortifying resistance against steganalysis.

ii. *Quantum Steganography:* The emerging discipline of quantum information theory presents intriguing possibilities for highly secure steganographic techniques, offering enhanced safeguarding for important intellectual property assets.

iii. *Standardisation and Regulation:* Cooperation among industry, legal scholars, and policymakers can result in the establishment of uniform steganographic techniques and explicit laws, guaranteeing responsible utilisation and legal enforceability.

11. Privacy and ethical considerations of steganography

Steganography, the practice of hiding messages behind seemingly harmless objects, is an effective means for ensuring secure communication and safeguarding data [36]. However, similar to any potent instrument, its utilisation gives rise to substantial privacy and ethical issues that necessitate meticulous deliberation. This chapter thoroughly examines the complex issues surrounding steganography, investigating the potential advantages and dangers it presents in different situations.

11.1 Balancing security and privacy

Steganography, as a technique, provides strong security advantages in many situations. However, its intrinsic concealment also gives rise to important privacy issues, necessitating a careful balancing of interests. To successfully navigate this complex process, one must carefully analyse the ethical, legal, and societal consequences of this highly influential technology [53].

Incorporating data into cover sources like as photographs or documents provides an additional level of security, potentially safeguarding confidential information from unauthorised access. Ensuring the safeguarding of personal information, commercial secrets, and confidential conversations is of utmost importance [5].

Issues related to the protection of personal information: Nevertheless, the act of hiding information might give rise to issues of privacy. Steganography, when employed without transparency or informed consent, can be exploited to conceal information from persons who are entitled to access it [21]. Employers who adopt steganography to clandestinely monitor employee communication infringe upon the privacy rights of their employees.

It is essential to strike an optimal equilibrium between security and privacy. Organisations that employ steganography must establish explicit policies and processes to ensure its ethical and transparent utilisation, while also respecting the privacy rights of individuals [35].

11.2 Ethical dilemmas and misuse

Steganography provides effective methods for ensuring secure communication and safeguarding data. However, its ability to hide information also raises important ethical concerns and the possibility of misuse [22]. It is essential to comprehend these significant issues in order to support responsible utilisation and reduce the potential dangers linked to this potent technology.

Key Dilemmas [12, 48, 49]:

i. *Surveillance and Censorship:* Steganography can be exploited for the purposes of monitoring and controlling information flow. Government entities or influential entities could employ it for clandestine surveillance of communications or to impose limitations on information accessibility, so compromising both freedom of speech and privacy rights.

ii. *Malicious Intent:* When used by individuals with nefarious intentions, steganography can enable illicit acts such as cybercrime, dissemination of false information, or concealing incriminating evidence. The improper use of this can result in significant repercussions, negatively impacting both individuals and society at large.

iii. *Ethical Obligation:* Developers and users of steganographic technologies bear a moral duty to ensure their responsible use and to avoid any exploitation for malevolent intentions. This necessitates transparency, strict compliance with legal requirements, and careful deliberation of the potential societal ramifications of their activities.

11.3 Legal landscape and regulatory challenges

Although the promise for secure communication and data security is unquestionable, the inherent secrecy presents intricate legal and regulatory obstacles [36]. Successfully navigating this intricate maze necessitates a sophisticated comprehension of current legislation, any legal gaps, and the ever-changing regulatory landscape.

11.3.1 Existing legal frameworks

i. *Legal Ambiguity:* The legal framework pertaining to steganography is sometimes unclear, exhibiting variations among different jurisdictions. Certain countries have explicit legislation governing its utilisation, whereas others provide just restricted direction. The lack of clarity in this situation can pose difficulties for law enforcement and give rise to apprehensions over the responsibility for any wrongful usage [38].

ii. *Balancing Detection and Privacy:* Achieving a balance between accurately detecting illicit utilisation of steganography and safeguarding personal privacy is a crucial task. Excessive and forceful detection techniques may violate privacy rights, whilst insufficient detection exposes society to the risks of misuse [37].

iii. *Collaboration Necessity:* To tackle the legal and regulatory obstacles related to steganography, it is imperative for policymakers, technological developers, and civil society organisations to collaborate. This partnership has the potential to promote responsible use, establish explicit directives, and guarantee that legal frameworks safeguard the interests of both security and privacy [53].

12. The future of steganography

The unquestionable potential of secure communication and data security warrants careful examination of ethical and legal problems as we negotiate its future trajectory.

Incorporating methods for transparency and traceability into steganographic techniques could effectively address privacy issues and promote responsible utilisation. This may entail the creation of techniques that generate traceable digital records or necessitate user authorization for the inclusion of information [18].

It is vital to raise public understanding about the possible benefits and drawbacks of steganography. Providing folks with knowledge about its functioning, prospective applications, and the significance of responsible usage helps cultivate a society that is more knowledgeable and watchful [20].

Continuous communication and cooperation among stakeholders, such as developers, policymakers, and the general public, are crucial to guarantee the responsible and ethical development of steganography. This will contribute to a digital future that prioritises security and privacy [22].

13. Conclusion

In its conclusion, this chapter provides a comprehensive analysis of the various uses of steganography in several sectors, with a particular focus on its significance in banking, healthcare, intellectual property, and organisational communication. It explores motivations, tactics, advantages, and difficulties, providing insight into the future prospects and consequences of this secretive craft. Steganography demonstrates its versatility by improving security in business transactions and protecting sensitive medical data. The significance of blockchain technology in the digital ecosystem is highlighted by its ability to protect intellectual property and enable discreet communication within organisations. Although there are promising elements, it is important to carefully analyse issues such as computing overhead, vulnerability to steganalysis, and legal and ethical concerns. The chapter presents a future scenario in which steganography becomes integrated with upcoming technologies, works along with AI and quantum information theory, and develops industry-wide norms for responsible utilisation.

Author details

Mahmud Ahmad Bamanga[1*], Aliyu Kamalu Babando[2] and Mohammed Ahmed Shehu[1]

1 Computer Science Department, Federal University of Lafia, Nasarawa State, Nigeria

2 Department of Computer Science, Taraba State Polytechnics-Nigeria, Nigeria

*Address all correspondence to: mahmud.bamanga@cmp.fulafia.edu.ng

References

[1] Merrill W, Ernst B, Mark BS. Steganography: Forensic, security, and legal issues. The Journal of Digital Forensics, Security and Law. 2008;**3**(2):18-34

[2] Aliyu KB, Bamanga MA. Data security using steganography. LC International Journal of STEM. 2023;**3**(4):12-24

[3] Curran K, Bailey K. An evaluation of image based steganography methods. International Journal of Digital Evidence. 2003;**2**(2):1-40

[4] Mustafa MT, Abdrahim HA, Rana SH, Siti SM. A literature review of various steganography methods. Journal of Theoretical and Applied Information Technology. 2022;**100**(5):1412-1427

[5] Huo L, Chen R, Wei J, Huang L. A high-capacity and high-security image steganography network based on chaotic mapping and generative adversarial networks. Applied Sciences. 2024;**14**(3):1225

[6] Kunhoth J, Subramanian N, Al-Maadeed S. Video steganography: Recent advances and challenges. Multimedia Tools and Applications. 2023;**82**(27):41943-41985

[7] Nazife C, Taner C, Onur O, Ahmet G, Sajjad N, Fatih S. Improved exploiting modification direction steganography for hexagonal image processing. Journal of King Saud University – Computer and Information Sciences. 2022;**34**(10):9273-9283

[8] Dang NT, Hans-Jürgen Z, Thi MCC. LSB data hiding in digital media: A survey. EAI Endorsed Transactions on Industrial Networks and Intelligent Systems. 2022;**5**(4):1-50

[9] Sudhanshi S, Umesh K. Review of transform domain techniques for image steganography. International Journal of Science and Research (IJSR). 2013;**4**(5):194-197

[10] Li X, Guo D, Qin C. Diversified cover selection for image steganography. Symmetry. 2023;**15**(11):2024. DOI: 10.3390/sym15112024

[11] Anandaprova M, Sumana K, Suvamoy C. A unique database synthesis technique for coverless data hiding. Journal of Visual Communication and Image Representation. 2023;**96**. DOI: 10.1016/j.jvcir.2023.103911

[12] Kuznetsov A, Onikiychuk A, Peshkova O, Gancarczyk T, Warwas K, Ziubina R. Direct spread spectrum technology for data hiding in audio. Sensors (Basel). 2022;**22**(9):3115. DOI: 10.3390/s22093115

[13] Prakash V, Williams A, Garg L, Savaglio C, Bawa S. Cloud and edge computing-based computer forensics: Challenges and open problems. Electronics. 2021;**10**(11):1229. DOI: 10.3390/electronics10111229

[14] Płachta M, Krzemień M, Szczypiorski K, Janicki A. Detection of image steganography using deep learning and ensemble classifiers. Electronics. 2022;**11**(10):1565. DOI: 10.3390/electronics11101565

[15] Nujud A, Sabah A. An overview of steganography through history. International Journal of Scientific Engineering and Science. 2021;**5**(2):41-44

[16] Central Intelligence Agency. CIA.gov Launches Mobile Site. Central Intelligence Agency. 2012. Available

from: https://www.dni.gov/index.php/newsroom/news-articles/news-articles-2012/594-cia-gov-launches-mobile-site

[17] Zhong X, Das A, Alrasheedi F, Tanvir A. A brief, in-depth survey of deep learning-based image watermarking. Applied Sciences. 2023;**13**(21):11852. DOI: 10.3390/app132111852

[18] Yang W, Wang S, Cui H, Tang Z, Li Y. A review of homomorphic encryption for privacy-preserving biometrics. Sensors (Basel). 2023;**23**(7):3566. DOI: 10.3390/s23073566

[19] Vilas BEC, Silva JDS, Figueiredo FAP. Artificial intelligence for channel estimation in multicarrier systems for B5G/6G communications: A survey. EURASIP Journal on Wireless Communications and Networking. 2022;**116**(1). DOI: 10.1186/s13638-022-02195-3

[20] Mustafa T, Naim A, Adem O, Taner D. OTA 2.0: An advanced and secure blockchain steganography algorithm. International Journal of Computational and Experimental Science and Engineering. 2023;**9**(4):419-434

[21] Padyab A, Ståhlbröst A. Privacy enhancing tools: A literature review on end user role and evaluation. In: Proceedings of the Eleventh International Symposium on Human Aspects of Information Security & Assurance (HAISA 2017). Adelaide, Australia; 2017. pp. 202-214. Available from: https://www.diva-portal.org/smash/get/diva2:1173944/FULLTEXT01.pdf

[22] What is steganography? By simplilearn. 2023. Available from: https://www.simplilearn.com/what-is-steganography-article#steganography_vs_cryptography

[23] Majeed MA, Sulaiman R, Shukur Z, Hasan MK. A review on text steganography techniques. Mathematics. 2021;**9**(21):2829. DOI: 10.3390/math9212829

[24] Abid H, Mohd J, Mohd AQ, Rajiv S. Understanding the role of digital technologies in education: A review. Sustainable Operations and Computers. 2022;**3**:275-285

[25] Kaspersky. What is steganography & how does it work? 2023. Available from: https://www.kaspersky.com/resource-center/definitions/what-is-steganography

[26] Kefa R. Steganography-the art of hiding data. Information Technology Journal. 2004;**3**(3):245-269

[27] Patricia B. A universal cybersecurity competency framework for organizational users [PhD thesis]. Nova Southeastern University; 2022

[28] Dinesh S, Shubham C, Madhavi J, Sagar B, Swapnali B, Jadhav SA. Online secure payment system using steganography and cryptography. International Journal of Advanced in Management, Technology and Engineering Sciences. 2017;**7**(12):71-75

[29] Khan M, Parvaiz GS, Dedahanov AT, Abdurazzakov OS, Rakhmonov DA. The impact of Technologies of Traceability and Transparency in supply chains. Sustainability. 2022;**14**(24):16336. DOI: 10.3390/su142416336

[30] Orucho D, Awuor F, Makiya R, Oduor C. Review of algorithms for securing data transmission in mobile banking. Modern Economy. 2023;**14**(9):1192-1217. DOI: 10.4236/me.2023.149062

[31] IBM. What is data security? Data security definition and overview – IBM. ibm.com. 2023. Available from: https://www.ibm.com/topics/data-security

[32] Hand DJ. Aspects of data ethics in a changing world: Where are we now? Big Data. 2018;**6**(3):176-190. DOI: 10.1089/big.2018.0083

[33] Jean-Paul AY, Hassan NN, Ola S, Ali C. Robotics cyber security: Vulnerabilities, attacks, countermeasures, and recommendations. International Journal of Information Security. 2022;**21**:115-158

[34] Daniel JK, Neha R, Andras S. Fortifying data security: A multifaceted approach with MFA, cryptography, and steganography. FMDB Transactions on Sustainable Computing Systems. 2023;**1**(2):98-111

[35] Su J, Zhu L, Peng S, Cai Z, Liu W, He C, et al. Research on privacy data protection based on trusted computing and blockchain. Security and Communication Networks. 2021;**2021**(9). DOI: 10.1155/2021/6274860

[36] Nguyen A, Ngo HN, Hong Y. Ethical principles for artificial intelligence in education. Education and Information Technologies. 2023;**28**:4221-4241. DOI: 10.1007/s10639-022-11316-w

[37] Avasthi A, Grover S, Nischal A. Ethical and legal issues in psychotherapy. Indian Journal of Psychiatry. 2022;**64**(1):47-S61

[38] Jean-Paul A, Yaacoub HN, Noura OS, Ali C. Ethical hacking for IoT: Security issues, challenges, solutions and recommendations. Internet of Things and Cyber-Physical Systems. 2023;**3**:280-308

[39] Gnanalakshmi V, Indumathi G. A review on image steganographic techniques based on optimization algorithms for secret communication. Multimedia Tools and Applications. 2023;**82**:44245-44258. DOI: 10.1007/s11042-023-15568-7

[40] Nawaz SA, Li J, Bhatti UA, Mehmood A, Shoukat MU, Bhatti MA. Advance hybrid medical watermarking algorithm using speeded up robust features and discrete cosine transform. PLoS One. 2020;**15**(6):e0232902. DOI: 10.1371/journal.pone.0232902

[41] Taleby AM, Li Q, Hou J, Rajput AR, Chen Y. Modern text hiding, text Steganalysis, and applications: A comparative analysis. Entropy. 2019;**21**(4):355. DOI: 10.3390/e21040355

[42] Mohammed SA, Rashidi CBM, Rifikha AAR, Safa SH. Digital image steganography in spatial domain a comprehensive review. Journal of Theoretical and Applied Information Technology. 2019;**97**(19):5081-5102

[43] Zheng X, Gildea E, Chai S, Zhang T, Wang S. Data science in finance: Challenges and opportunities. AI. 2024;**5**(1):55-71. DOI: 10.3390/ai5010004

[44] Caviglione L. Trends and challenges in network covert channels countermeasures. Applied Sciences. 2021;**11**(4):1641. DOI: 10.3390/app11041641

[45] Shehab DA, Alhaddad MJ. Comprehensive survey of multimedia Steganalysis: Techniques, evaluations, and trends in future research. Symmetry. 2022;**14**(1):117. DOI: 10.3390/sym14010117

[46] Seh AH, Zarour M, Alenezi M, et al. Healthcare data breaches: Insights and implications. Healthcare (Basel). 2020;**8**(2):133. DOI: 10.3390/healthcare8020133

[47] Yelne S, Chaudhary M, Dod K, Sayyad A, Sharma R. Harnessing the power of AI: A comprehensive review of its impact and challenges in nursing science and healthcare. Cureus. 2023;**15**(11):e49252. DOI: 10.7759/cureus.49252

[48] AlEisa HN. Data confidentiality in healthcare monitoring systems based on image steganography to improve the exchange of patient information using the internet of things. Journal of Healthcare Engineering. 2022;**2022**:7528583. DOI: 10.1155/2022/7528583

[49] Magdy M, Hosny KM, Ghali NI, Ghoniemy S. Security of medical images for telemedicine: A systematic review. Multimedia Tools and Applications. 2022;**81**(18):25101-25145. DOI: 10.1007/s11042-022-11956-7

[50] Shafiq M, Gu Z. Deep residual learning for image recognition: A survey. Applied Sciences. 2022;**12**(18):8972. DOI: 10.3390/app12188972

[51] Zeng L, Yang N, Li X, Chen A, Jing H, Zhang J. Advanced image steganography using a U-Net-based architecture with multi-scale fusion and perceptual loss. Electronics. 2023;**12**(18):3808. DOI: 10.3390/electronics12183808

[52] Liu Y, Zhang J, Wu S, Pathan MS. Research on digital copyright protection based on the hyperledger fabric blockchain network technology. Peer Journal of Computer Science. 2021;**7**:e709. DOI: 10.7717/peerj-cs.709

[53] Kendal E. Ethical, legal and social implications of emerging technology (ELSIET) symposium. Journal of Bioethics Inquality. 2022;**19**(3):363-370. DOI: 10.1007/s11673-022-10197-5

Chapter 3

Steganography: Unveiling Techniques and Research Agenda

Arvind Kumar Op Dangi, Stuti Tandon, Shalesh Deorari and Rajeev Kumar

Abstract

Steganography techniques focus on command-based and tool-based approaches for concealing digital information within diverse media formats. This study analyzes the functionalities of methodologies, implementation intricacies, and their potential advancements. Examining the intricacies of command-based steganography elucidates the intricate process of concealing data within digital files using terminal commands, thereby highlighting the Least Significant Bit (LSB) technique through command-line operations. This study highlights functionalities and user interfaces of prominent steganography tools, such as Steghide and OpenStego, thereby emphasizing ease of use and graphical capabilities for embedding and extracting hidden data. The comparative analysis assesses the strengths and limitations of methods, outlining the granular control offered by command-based steganography against the user-friendliness of tool-based approaches. The research delineates future scope and challenges in advancing steganographic techniques, envisaging advancements in algorithmic robustness, cross-platform compatibility, and integration with emerging technologies. Limitations pertaining to data capacity, file compatibility, and detection risks are acknowledged to provide insights into areas necessitating further research and development. The study culminates potential implementation scenarios for command-based and tool-based steganography. The research findings serve as a valuable resource for practitioners, researchers, and stakeholders seeking to comprehend, implement, and innovate steganographic methodologies in contemporary digital environments.

Keywords: steganography, blockchain, fusion, steganographic techniques, information security

1. Introduction

Steganography, derived from the Greek words "steganos" (significance hidden or covered) and "graphy" (significance composing or drawing), is an old artistry that has established into a sophisticated science in the age of technology. Steganography uniquely hides the data by embedding it in unnoticeable containers to enable secret interactions [1]. This training traces back to antiquated developments, where mystery messages were concealed in different structures, like undetectable ink on the material.

However, with the approach of computerized innovations, steganography has tracked down new applications and has turned into a vital part of the domain of data forensics and cybersecurity [2, 3].

The roots of steganography can be traced back to the age of early human civilizations when individuals sought to carefully exchange secret information [2]. One outstanding authentic model is the undetectable ink by old Greeks and Romans to pass on secret messages. By heating or adding additional compounds to the seemingly transparent material, its intended recipient would be able to unravel the hidden message. During the Middle Ages, imperceptible composing procedures were developed with professionals utilizing substances like lemon squeeze or milk to make stowed-away messages. During seasons of war, undetectable ink turned into an important device for the military, permitting messages to be sent clandestinely.

In the age of digital technology and the Internet, steganography includes implanting data inside advanced records, for example, pictures, sound records, recordings, and even text reports [4]. This is executed in such a manner that it is nearly impossible for a normal human to find out the cipher information without particular devices, tools, or strategies [5]. Throughout the epochs of human communication, the enigmatic art of steganography has etched its presence, an elusive dance of concealment and revelation that transcends the pages of history. In the mosaic of clandestine messaging, steganography is the subtle brushstroke, an ancient practice shrouded in the veils of secrecy. Its origins can be traced back to the cryptic corridors of ancient civilizations, where inventive minds sought to transmit confidential information through covert means. The Greeks and Romans, masters of intrigue, wielded invisible ink to inscribe hidden messages upon the parchment, a veil lifted only by the alchemy of heat or the touch of specific substances. These early forays into the realm of secret communication set the stage for steganography's enduring journey [6]. The medieval tapestry unfolded with new chapters in the art of hidden writing. Ingenious methods emerged, with practitioners employing substances like lemon juice or milk to create concealed missives. The quest for secrecy extended to the Renaissance era, where courts buzzed with intrigue, and steganography became an indispensable tool for those navigating the delicate dance of power and diplomacy. Letters became vessels for concealed information, with invisible writing techniques taking center stage [7]. Secret compartments and concealed compartments within letters and documents concealed coded messages, adding layers of complexity to the covert exchange of information.

As the sands of time flowed, steganography metamorphosed in tandem with the evolution of societies and technologies. The dawn of the digital age heralded a new chapter, as ancient methods found resonance in the realm of pixels and bytes. In this contemporary context, steganography is no longer confined to ink and parchment but extends its subtle tendrils into the digital landscape. Images, audio files, and even text serve as carriers for concealed information, with techniques like least significant bit (LSB) replacement and frequency domain transformations becoming the modern artisan's tools [8].

The historical narrative of steganography is an intricate tapestry woven with threads of secrecy and innovation. Its continued relevance in the digital age underscores its timeless appeal as a means of secure communication. The journey of steganography, from ancient civilizations to the present day, is a testament to the human inclination to safeguard information through artful concealment [9]. In the clandestine corridors of espionage, steganography emerged as a silent ally, a trusted confidant for those navigating the intricacies of war and diplomacy. Military leaders and intelligence operatives recognized the potency of concealed messages in shaping the outcomes of battles. Steganography became a covert weapon, allowing generals to communicate strategic plans beyond enemy lines without arousing suspicion. The artistry of hidden writing became an integral part of military strategy, a secret language shared among the known connected parties. The Renaissance era witnessed steganography's ascent to new heights of sophistication. In an age where courts were rife with political machinations and intrigues, the ability to convey messages discreetly held immense value. Secret compartments within letters, invisible inks, and coded symbols adorned missives exchanged by diplomats, statesmen, and monarchs. Steganography became the trusted companion of those navigating the delicate dance of diplomacy, enabling the conveyance of confidential information beneath the veneer of ordinary communication. As societies traversed the tapestry of time, steganography continued to evolve, embracing the challenges and opportunities presented by emerging technologies. The advent of the telegraph and Morse code opened new frontiers for hidden communication. The rhythmic dots and dashes of Morse code became a canvas for coded messages, concealing intent within the seemingly mundane. Steganography adapted to the telegraph's staccato language, offering a clandestine means of communication that spanned vast distances. The digital revolution of the late twentieth century ushered in a new era for steganography. As the world transitioned from analog to digital, the practice found new avenues for expression. The advent of computers and the proliferation of digital media expanded steganography's repertoire [10]. Images became the modern parchment, and digital files the canvas for concealed messages. Techniques like LSB replacement allowed information to be hidden within the binary code of images, imperceptible to the human eye but retrievable by those privy to the key. In the labyrinth of the Internet, steganography found fertile ground. The interconnected web of networks provided a vast canvas for covert communication. Steganography became a tool for those navigating the complexities of cybersecurity and digital forensics [2]. Cybercriminals and hackers leveraged steganographic techniques to conceal malware, exfiltrate data, and orchestrate covert communication within the vast expanse of the digital realm. In the contemporary landscape, steganography is a multifaceted art, finding applications across diverse domains. Its role extends beyond espionage and military strategy to encompass areas such as cybersecurity, digital forensics, and even art and entertainment. The subtle dance of concealment and revelation that defines steganography continues to captivate minds in an age where information is both a currency and a vulnerability. As we reflect on the intricate history of steganography, it becomes evident that its allure lies not only in its ability to safeguard information but also in its status as a timeless expression of human ingenuity [3]. From the clandestine corridors of ancient civilizations to the digital realm of the twenty-first century, steganography has persevered, adapting and innovating in response to the evolving needs of societies. It is a testament to the indomitable human spirit that seeks to navigate the delicate balance between secrecy and revelation, a dance that transcends the confines of time and technology.

2. History of steganography

The principle of the use of steganography traces back to the Greeks. Herodotus tells how a message was passed to the Greeks about Xerses' threatening expectations under the wax of a composing tablet and depicts a procedure of specking progressive letters in a cover message with a mystery ink, because of Aeneas the Tactician. Pirate legends recount the act of inking restricted data, like a guide, on the head of somebody, so the hair would disguise it. Kahn recounts a stunt used in China of implanting a code ideogram at a setup position in a dispatch; a comparative thought prompted the grille framework used in middle-aged Europe, where a wooden layout would be set over a harmless message, featuring an implanted mystery message. During World War, II the grille technique or a few variations were used by spies. In a similar period, the Germans created microdot innovation, which prints a reasonable, great quality photo contracting it to the size of a dot. There are bits of hearsay that during the 1980s, Margareth Thatcher, then, at that point, Head of the state in the UK, turned out to be so bothered about press holes of bureau records that she had the word processors modified to encode the personality of the essayist in the word dividing, subsequently having the option to follow the backstabbing ministers. During the "Cool Conflict" period, the US and USSR needed to conceal their sensors in the foe's offices. These gadgets needed to send information to their countries, without being spotted. Today, steganography is explored both for legal and illegal reasons. Among the initial ones, there is war broadcast communications, which use spread range or meteor dissipate radio to disguise both the message and its source. In the business market, with the appearance of advanced interchanges and capacity, one of the main issues is copyright implementation, so computerized watermarking procedures are being created to confine the use of protected data [11]. Another significant use is to insert information about clinical pictures, so everything is good to go with matching patient's records and images. Among illegal ones is the act of stowing away firmly scrambled information to stay away from controls by cryptography trade regulations.

3. Working and uses of steganography

Steganography works by hiding data in a manner that evades doubt [12]. One of the most pervasive procedures is called "least significant bit" (LSB) steganography. This includes implanting the desired data in the least significant bits of a document. For instance:

- In an image, every pixel is comprised of three bytes compared to the varieties red, green, and blue. Some image designs utilize an additional "alpha" fourth byte.

- LSB steganography changes the last bit of every one of those bytes to cover up the slightest bit of information. Along these lines, to conceal one megabyte of information utilizing this technique, you would require an eight-megabyte image.

- Altering the last bit of the pixel does not bring any outwardly discernible change to the image and that implies that anybody seeing the original and the steganographic image [13] would not be able to differentiate.

Similar techniques can be applied to other media, like sound and video, where information is concealed in pieces of the file that do not reveal the changes and make it look like a normal file [8]. Another steganography method is the use of word or letter substitution [14]. This is where the cipher message is hidden in the data by merging it inside a bigger message, putting the words at explicit spans. While this substitution strategy is not difficult to use, it might make the message look bizarre and awkward since the cipher texts do not make any sense within their objective sentences. Other steganography techniques include concealing a whole segment for a hard drive or implanting information in the header part of records and organization bundles. The effectiveness of these techniques relies heavily on how much information they can stow away and that they are so natural to identify. There are different uses of steganography as depicted in **Figure 1** which are listed below:

- Steganography can be a kind of solution that can provide a way to share data and information between communicating and concerned parties without any worries.

- It is relevant to just use steganography to save information in an area. For instance, a few data sources like the confidential financial data, a few military mysteries can be saved in a cover source. When it is expected to uncover the restricted information in the cover source, it reveals only the financial information, and is impossible to accept that there are tactical puzzles within.

- Steganography can be for the most part used to perform watermarking. Albeit the idea of watermarking is not certainly steganography [12]. A few steganographic approaches are being used to save watermarks in information. The significant distinction is on settled, while the aim of steganography is concealing information [15], watermarking is scarcely expanding the cover source with additional information because individuals [16] will not acknowledge observable changes in pictures, sound, or video records because of a watermark, the steganographic approach can be used to disguise this.

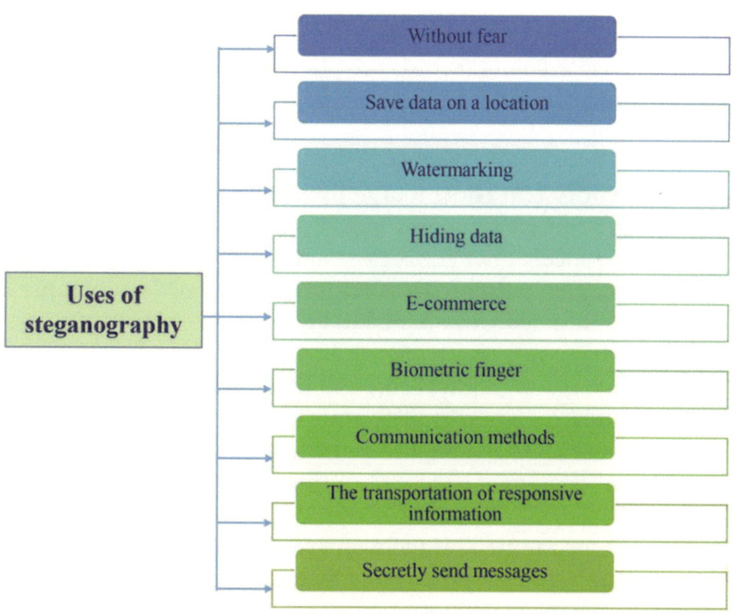

Figure 1.
Uses of steganography.

- Internet business empowers for a need of steganography. In current web-based business exchanges, users have their authentication ID and passwords, but this is not a genuine methodology for authenticating that the user is the real card holder. In analysing a biometric unique mark which has explicit meeting, IDs are introduced into the finger impression. It can empower an extremely safe decision to open an online business exchange confirmation [11].

- It very well may be paired with current specialized strategies; steganography can be used to achieve stowed-away trades. States are keen on two sorts of secret correspondences: those that help public safety and those that do not. Computerized steganography holds huge concealed for both the kinds. Organizations may face issues regarding exchanging privileged insights or new item information.

- The transportation of responsive data is one more key use of steganography. An expected issue with cryptography is that snoops understand they have a scrambled message when they inspect one. Steganography empowers responsive data by passing the busy bodies without any information about the responsive data. The idea of involving steganography in information transportation can be used to just about any information transportation approach, from Email to pictures on Web sites.

- The significant uses of steganography are that it tends to be used to furtively send messages without the reality of the transmission being found. Steganography is a methodology that improves on stowing away a message that will be maintained secret within other messages. This outcome is the mystery of the secret message itself. The steganography approach can be used for pictures, video documents, or sound recordings.

The use of steganography, such as watermarking, conceals copyright information inside a watermark by overlaying records not effectively concocted by the unaided eye. This evades deceitful activities and gives copyright media more insurance.

4. Steganography tools and their usage process

Steganography, the specialty of concealing data within different information or media, keeps on developing with progressions in innovation. Several types of steganography patterns and methods are depicted in **Figure 2**:

1. Deep learning in steganography: Profound brain networks have been used to make more modern steganographic strategies. Methods like generative adversarial networks (GANs) are utilized to create subtle modifications in pictures or sound, making it harder to distinguish stowed-away data.

2. Adversarial steganography: This includes creating strategies to conceal data that is impervious to recognition by enemy calculations. Adversarial training is used to make steganographic strategies that are powerful against recognition endeavors utilizing machine learning calculations.

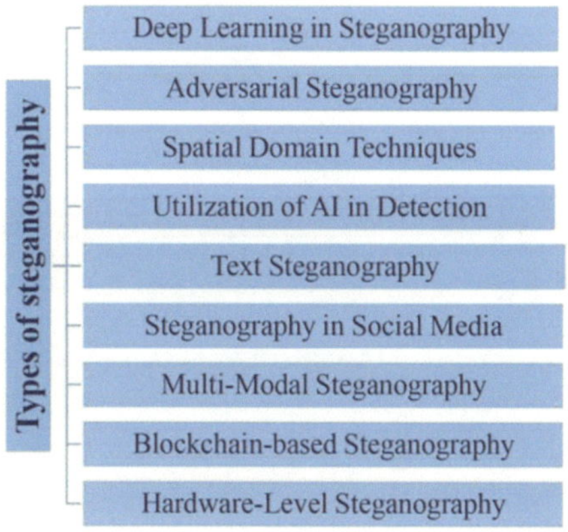

Figure 2.
Types of steganography.

3. Spatial domain methods: Late improvements center on spatial domain strategies, where changes are made straightforwardly to the pixels of a picture, sound, or video. Techniques like least significant bit (LSB) substitution have been refined to install information all the more productively while maintaining visual or hearable quality.

4. Utilization of AI in identification: As steganography strategies advance, so do the techniques to distinguish stowed-away data. AI and machine learning calculations are being utilized to recognize irregularities in information, utilizing factual examination, profound learning, and example acknowledgment to distinguish dubious substance.

5. Text steganography: Disguising data within text has gained consideration. Procedures like utilizing equivalent word substitution, arranging control, or even undetectable ink-style strategies in computerized text have been investigated.

6. Steganography in web-based entertainment: With the broad use of virtual entertainment stages, there is a developing interest in steganography for concealing data within pictures, recordings, or even remarks on these stages. Methods aim to insert information without apparently modifying the media to sidestep content channels.

7. Multi-modular steganography: This includes concealing data across various sorts of media. For example, implanting information in both a picture and a sound record all the while to build the volume of stowed-away data and make location testing.

8. Blockchain-based steganography: Coordinating steganography strategies with blockchain innovation for secure and undercover correspondence has been investigated, considering stowed-away informing within the blockchain information structure.

9. Hardware-level steganography: Investigating ways of inserting information within equipment parts, similar to CPUs or electronic circuits, presents new difficulties and amazing open doors for undercover correspondence.

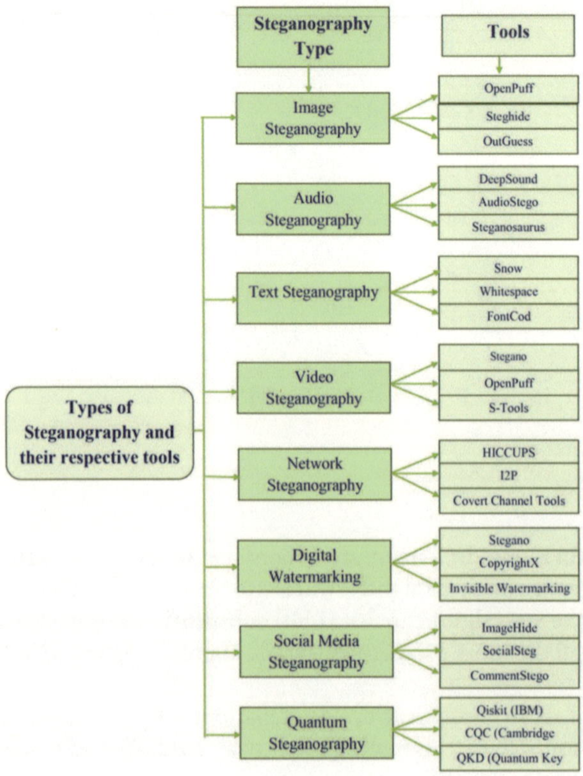

Figure 3.
Types of steganography and their respective tools.

Several types of steganography with their relevant tools have been depicted by **Figure 3**. The usage of these tools is important to explore steganography. The classified type of steganography, its relevant tool, and its usage process have been tabulated in **Table 1**.

4.1 Image steganography

4.1.1 OpenPuff

Description: OpenPuff is an open-source steganography device that supports various formats, including images, audio, and video. It employs transporter files, such as images, to securely conceal information [17].

Usage process: Select a cover image, choose the information to stow away, set encryption/password, and execute the inserting process.

4.1.2 Steghide

Description: Steghide is a command-line device that specializes in concealing information in various types of media files, including images. It uses robust algorithms for installation and extraction.

Usage process: Select a cover image, choose the information to stow away, set encryption/password, and execute the installing process.

S. No	Steganography type	Tools	Usage process
1	Image steganography	• OpenPuff	1. Select a cover image.
		• Steghide	2. Choose data to hide.
		• OutGuess	3. Set encryption/password.
			4. Execute embedding process.
2	Audio steganography	• DeepSound	1. Select an audio file.
		• AudioStego	2. Choose data to hide.
		• Steganosaurus	3. Set encryption/password.
			4. Execute embedding process.
3	Text steganography	• Snow	1. Input cover text.
		• Whitespace steganography	2. Enter data to hide.
		• FontCode	3. Set encryption/password.
			4. Execute embedding process.
4	Video steganography	• Stegano	1. Choose a video file.
		• OpenPuff	2. Select data to hide.
		• S-Tools	3. Set encryption/password.
			4. Execute embedding process.
5	Network steganography	• HICCUPS	1. Establish a communication channel.
		• I2P	2. Configure network steganography settings.
		• Covert channel tools	3. Implement data hiding within network packets.
			4. Ensure secure and authorized communication.
6	Digital watermarking	• Stegano	1. Choose a digital asset.
		• CopyrightX	2. Embed a watermark (data) into the asset.
		• Invisible watermarking	3. Adjust transparency and visibility settings.
			4. Verify and authenticate watermarked digital assets.
7	Social media steganography	• ImageHide	1. Upload an image to a social media platform.
		• SocialSteg	2. Embed data within the image.
		• CommentStego	3. Post the image with hidden information.
			4. Share securely on social media for covert communication.
8	Quantum steganography	• Qiskit (IBM)	1. Encode quantum information into qubits.
		• CQC (Cambridge Quantum Computing)	2. Utilize quantum gates for embedding.
		• QKD (quantum key distribution)	3. Apply quantum principles for secure communication.
			4. Employ quantum entanglement for covert transmission.

Table 1.
Types of steganography, tools, and usage process.

4.1.3 OutGuess

Description: OutGuess is a steganography device that focuses on concealing information in images. It aims to maintain the visual nature of the image while implanting information in the least significant bits.

Usage process: Select a cover image, choose the information to stow away, set encryption/password, and execute the installing process.

4.2 Audio steganography

4.2.1 DeepSound

Description: DeepSound is a Windows-based steganography device that hides information in audio files. It uses recurrence domain techniques to install information, ensuring an insignificant effect on audio quality.

Usage process: Select an audio document, choose the information to stow away, set encryption/password, and execute the inserting process.

4.2.2 AudioStego

Description: AudioStego is an open-source device that allows users to conceal information in audio files. It employs various inserting techniques, such as LSB control, to disguise information.

Usage process: Select an audio document, choose the information to stow away, set encryption/password, and execute the installing process.

4.2.3 Steganosaurus

Description: Steganosaurus is a Python-based steganography instrument for audio files. It focuses on concealing information within the audio signal, giving a covert channel to communication.

Usage process: Select an audio record, choose the information to stow away, set encryption/password, and execute the inserting process.

4.3 Text steganography

4.3.1 Snow

Description: Snow is a steganography device that hides messages in whitespace characters within a text record. It is a simple and lightweight instrument for text-based communication.

Usage process: Info cover text, enter information to stow away, set encryption/password, and execute the installing process.

4.3.2 Whitespace steganography

Description: Whitespace steganography involves concealing information within the whitespace characters of a text record. It tends to be accomplished using various encoding methods.

Usage process: Enter information to stow away, set encryption/password, and execute the inserting process.

4.3.3 FontCode

Description: FontCode is a steganography method that hides information within the shapes of characters in a text report. It subtly alters the shapes of characters to encode information.

Usage process: Information cover text, enter information to stow away, set encryption/password, and execute the implanting process.

4.4 Video steganography

4.4.1 Stegano

Description: Stegano is a Python library that allows users to conceal information in video files. It provides a platform-free solution for implanting information in video streams.

Usage process: Choose a video document, select information to stow away, set encryption/password, and execute the installing process.

4.4.2 OpenPuff (video module)

Description: OpenPuff also supports video steganography. It extends its capabilities to conceal information within video files securely.

Usage process: Choose a video record, select information to stow away, set encryption/password, and execute the inserting process.

4.4.3 S-Tools

Description: S-Tools is a software suite that includes tools for concealing information in various types of media, including images and videos. It provides encryption options for secure information stowing away.

Usage process: Choose a video record, select information to stow away, set encryption/password, and execute the installing process.

4.5 Network steganography

4.5.1 HICCUPS

Description: Hidden Communication System for Corrupted Networks (HICCUPS) is a network steganography device designed to work over untrustworthy and corrupted networks.

Usage process: Establish a communication channel, design network steganography settings, carry out information stowing away within network packets, and ensure secure and approved communication.

4.5.2 I2P

Description: Invisible Internet Project (I2P) is an anonymous network layer that allows for secure and confidential communication. It tends to be used for covert communication within the I2P network.

Usage process: Arrange network steganography settings, execute information stowing away within network packets, and ensure secure and approved communication.

4.5.3 Covert channel tools

Description: Covert channel tools encompass various techniques and tools that work with communication over network channels while remaining undetected by security measures.

Usage process: Carry out information stowing away within network packets using specific covert channel techniques, ensuring secure and approved communication.

4.6 Digital watermarking

4.6.1 Stegano (digital watermarking module)

Description: Stegano is a versatile Python library that supports digital watermarking. It allows users to insert and concentrate watermarks from various types of digital assets.

Usage process: Choose a digital asset, insert a watermark (information) into the asset, adjust transparency and visibility settings, and check and validate watermarked digital assets.

4.6.2 CopyrightX

Description: CopyrightX is a device that facilitates the installing of digital watermarks into multimedia files. It adds a novel identifier to the substance to safeguard licensed innovation.

Usage process: Choose a digital asset, implant a watermark (information) into the asset, adjust transparency and visibility settings, and check and verify watermarked digital assets.

4.6.3 Invisible watermarking

Description: Invisible watermarking involves implanting a watermark into a digital substance in a manner that is vague to human senses [18]. It is usually used for copyright assurance.

Usage process: Install a watermark (information) into the digital asset, adjust transparency and visibility settings, and check and verify watermarked digital assets.

4.7 Social media steganography

4.7.1 ImageHide

Description: ImageHide is a steganography device designed for concealing information within images. It tends to be used for covert communication on social media platforms.

Usage process: Transfer an image to a social media platform, insert information within the image, post the image with hidden information, and share securely on social media.

4.7.2 SocialSteg

Description: SocialSteg is a steganography instrument specifically created for hiding information within images planned for social media sharing. It focuses on simplicity and ease of use.

Usage process: Transfer an image to a social media platform, insert information within the image, post the image with hidden information, and share securely on social media.

4.7.3 CommentStego

Description: CommentStego involves concealing information within comments or captions on social media platforms. It allows for covert communication within the text going with shared content.

Usage process: Post an image with hidden information, integrate information into comments or captions, and share securely on social media.

4.8 Quantum steganography

4.8.1 Qiskit (IBM)

Description: Qiskit is an open-source quantum computing software improvement structure given by IBM. It includes tools for quantum programming and allows for encoding quantum information into qubits.

Usage process: Encode quantum information into qubits, use quantum gates for inserting, apply quantum principles for secure communication, and utilize quantum snare for covert transmission.

4.8.2 Cambridge Quantum Computing (CQC)

Description: CQC provides quantum solutions, including quantum key distribution (QKD) and quantum-safe communication. It supports quantum steganography by using quantum principles for secure communication.

Usage process: Carry out quantum principles for secure communication and utilize quantum snare for covert transmission.

4.8.3 Quantum key distribution (QKD)

Description: Quantum key distribution (QKD) involves using quantum principles to secure communication channels. It ensures the respectability and privacy of transmitted information.

Usage process: Apply quantum key distribution principles to establish secure communication channels and use quantum snare for covert transmission.

5. Real-time applications of steganography techniques

5.1 Image steganography

5.1.1 Real-time application secure communication in images

Description: Image steganography is usually used for secure communication where sensitive information needs to be transmitted discreetly. In real-time applications, this could involve sending secret information through image attachments in emails or through image uploads in messaging apps, ensuring that the communication remains inconspicuous.

5.1.2 Real-time application copyright protection

Description: Digital watermarks inserted using image steganography can be used for copyright protection. In real time, photographers and artists can implant invisible watermarks in their images to claim ownership. This helps in tracking and proving ownership if the images are used without approval.

5.2 Audio steganography

5.2.1 Real-time application covert communication in VoIP calls

Description: Audio steganography can be applied in real-time communication, especially in voice over Internet protocol (VoIP) calls. Concealing information within audio signals allows for covert communication during voice calls, making it challenging for eavesdroppers to distinguish hidden information.

5.2.2 Real-time application music streaming with hidden messages

Description: In the context of music streaming services, audio steganography can be utilized to implant hidden messages within songs. Artists or content creators could use this method to share exclusive content, messages, or promotions with their crowd without altering the listening experience.

5.3 Text steganography

5.3.1 Real-time application secure chat communication

Description: Text steganography can be applied in real-time chat applications to ensure secure communication. Users can conceal sensitive information within ordinary text messages, providing a layer of privacy during instant messaging.

5.3.2 Real-time application covert communication in social media posts

Description: Social media platforms often screen content for various reasons, however, text steganography can be utilized to include hidden messages in public posts. Users can share information covertly within the text of their updates, allowing for discreet communication.

5.4 Video steganography

5.4.1 Real-time application secure video conferencing

Description: Video steganography can be used in real-time video conferencing for secure communication. Participants can insert extra information within video streams, ensuring private information trade during business meetings or sensitive discussions.

5.4.2 Real-time application hidden information in multimedia content

Description: In multimedia sharing platforms, users can utilize video steganography to implant hidden messages or extra content within videos. This could be used for promotions, exclusive content sharing, or artistic expression without altering the general viewing experience.

5.5 Network steganography

5.5.1 Real-time application covert communication in Internet traffic

Description: Network steganography can be used in real time to accomplish covert communication within Internet traffic. This method can assist in bypassing with networking surveillance or censorship, allowing users to trade information without raising suspicion.

5.5.2 Real-time application secure communication in VPNs

Description: In virtual private networks (VPNs), network steganography can improve security by embedding information within the scrambled traffic. This helps in achieving secure communication channels while making it challenging for adversaries to recognize hidden information.

5.6 Digital watermarking

5.6.1 Real-time application copyright protection in streaming services

Description: Digital watermarking is utilized in real time for copyright protection in streaming services. Content providers can implant invisible watermarks in streaming videos, ensuring that their ownership is recognized and protected against unapproved distribution.

5.6.2 Real-time application authentication in document sharing

Description: Digital watermarking can be used in real time for document authentication during sharing. Users can implant watermarks in sensitive documents to ensure legitimacy and track the source if unapproved distribution occurs.

5.7 Social media steganography

5.7.1 Real-time application covert communication in public posts

Description: Social media steganography is applied in real time to include hidden messages within public posts. Users can share information, links, or other content discreetly within the images or captions of their public posts.

5.7.2 Real-time application secure image sharing

Description: In real-time image sharing on social media, users can utilize image steganography to conceal extra information within images. This can be used for private messages or sharing classified details in a seemingly innocuous image.

5.8 Quantum steganography

5.8.1 Real-time application quantum-secure communication

Description: Quantum steganography can be applied in real time for secure communication using quantum principles. Quantum key distribution and trap-based techniques give an elevated degree of security, making it challenging for adversaries to intercept or identify hidden information.

5.8.2 Real-time application quantum-secure messaging

Description: In real-time messaging systems, quantum steganography can ensure secure communication by leveraging quantum snare for covert transmission. This can be especially useful in scenarios where classical encryption methods might be powerless against quantum attacks.

6. Role of steganography in different industries

Steganography plays a significant role in various industries, contributing to secure communication, information protection, and authentication. Here is an outline of its uses in various sectors (**Figure 4**).

6.1 Cybersecurity

Steganography is utilized as a cybersecurity measure to cover sensitive information, making it harder for unapproved parties to distinguish or intercept critical information. It helps in secure communication and prevents information spillage during transmission.

6.2 Military and defense

In military and defense applications, steganography is used to securely transmit classified information and maintain the privacy of sensitive information [19]. It aids in covert communication, ensuring that critical messages remain hidden from adversaries.

6.3 Law enforcement

Law enforcement agencies use steganography to reveal hidden information in digital proof. It plays a pivotal in digital forensics, helping investigators recognize covert communications, hidden messages, or hidden information in multimedia files.

6.4 Healthcare

Steganography can be applied in healthcare to secure the transmission of patient records, clinical images, and other sensitive information. It ensures patient security and helps in maintaining the privacy of healthcare information.

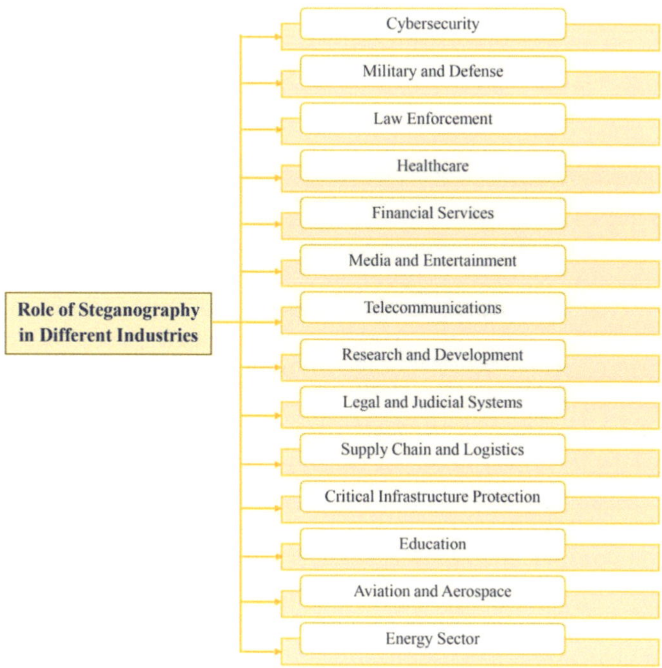

Figure 4.
Role of steganography in different industries.

6.5 Financial services

In the financial sector, steganography is used for secure communication in online banking, financial transactions, and information sharing between institutions. It helps shield financial information from unapproved access and interception.

6.6 Media and entertainment

Steganography is utilized in the media and entertainment industry for digital watermarking to safeguard intellectual property rights. It helps in embedding invisible watermarks in multimedia content, such as images, audio, and videos.

6.7 Telecommunications

Telecommunication companies use steganography to secure voice and information communication. It aids in preventing eavesdropping and unapproved interception of information, especially in voice over Internet protocol (VoIP) calls and messaging services.

6.8 Research and development

In research and development, steganography can be used to safeguard intellectual property, research findings, and exclusive information. It helps organizations maintain an upper hand by securing sensitive information.

6.9 Legal and judicial systems

Steganography plays a vital role in legal and judicial systems during investigations and court proceedings. It assists in uncovering hidden proof, verifying the validity of digital documents, and ensuring the integrity of electronic records.

6.10 Supply chain and logistics

In supply chain and logistics, steganography can be utilized to secure communication and information trade among various stakeholders. It ensures the secrecy of shipping information, inventory information, and transaction details.

6.11 Critical infrastructure protection

Steganography is used to upgrade the security of critical infrastructure systems, such as power grids and transportation networks. It helps in securing communication channels and protecting sensitive information connected with infrastructure operations.

6.12 Education

Educational institutions can use steganography to securely transmit sensitive information, maintain information integrity, and safeguard scholarly records. It contributes to secure communication in research collaborations and scholarly information trade.

6.13 Aviation and aerospace

In the aviation and aerospace industry, steganography is applied to secure communication channels connected with flight information, route systems, and aircraft communications. It helps safeguard critical information from digital threats.

6.14 Energy sector

The energy sector utilizes steganography to safeguard communication within the industry. It plays a vital role in securing information connected with energy creation, distribution, and monitoring systems.

7. Advantages and disadvantages of steganography

The upside of steganography is as per the following:

- The upside of steganography is that messages do not send thoughts to themselves. Perceptible scrambled messages, regardless of how extreme, will animate doubt and may in themselves be compromising in nations where encryption is ill-conceived.
- In steganography, cryptography gets the items in a message, steganography can be said to get the two messages and associating parties.

- This approach highlighted security, limit, and robustness, the three required components of steganography that make it useful in the secret trade of information through text records and making secret correspondence.

- There are a few significant records conveying secret information that can be in the server in an encoded structure and no gatecrasher can get some helpful data from the underlying document during communication.

- With the need for Steganography organization, government and policing can associate secretly.

- The goal of steganography is to interface secretly in a subtle viewpoint and to forestall attracting uncertainty to the transmission of secret data [12]. It is not to prevent others from understanding the secret information, however, it is to keep others from feeling that the information even exists. If a steganography approach creates somebody to think of the transporter medium, in this manner, the technique is fruitless.

- The upside of steganography is that it very well may be for the most part used to furtively send messages without the instance of the transmission being found. By utilizing encryption, it can perceive the source and the recipient.

- Steganography has a twofold part of security, for example, first, the actual document is confidential, and second, the information in it is encoded.

Several drawbacks of steganography are reported as:

- There is an enormous number of data and a large document size, large enough to be noticed.

- If this approach is gone in malicious hands, for example, programmers, fear mongers, and lawbreakers, then this can be especially basic to implement.

- Steganography is not without its drawbacks. Nonetheless, these can be redressed whenever it is performed and it can fortify the component of steganography.

- Most information concealing methodologies exploit human perceptual inadequacy, yet they lack of their own. These can be autonomously rectified.

- Algorithmically it is not much sound as compared to cryptography.

8. Future headings and arising patterns

The future of steganography is interlaced with innovative headways and arising patterns. As innovation advances, steganography is likely going to continue to adjust to new difficulties and entryways.

8.1 Quantum steganography

Quantum steganography is an emerging field that investigates the use of quantum standards for secure correspondence. Quantum ensnarement and superposition offer noteworthy entryways for covering and communicating information in a quantum environment.

8.2 Blockchain integration

The integration of steganography with blockchain innovation is gaining popularity. Blockchain can give a decentralized and change safe record for steganographic keys and approval, which will help in improving security.

8.3 Dynamic and versatile procedures

Future steganographic procedures are supposed to be more one-of-a-kind and versatile, changing their strategies to advancing recognizable proof methods. This versatility aims to maintain the possibility of steganography notwithstanding headways in steganalysis.

8.4 Robustness against adversarial attacks

Specialists are chipping away at creating steganographic strategies that are strong against adversarial attacks. This includes upgrading the adaptability of steganographic frameworks against conscious endeavors to beat the concealing system.

8.5 Integration with AI and machine learning

The integration of steganography with Artificial Intelligence and machine learning will presumably provoke more present-day and useful disguise strategies. These frameworks could adjust to the changing landscape of ID strategies.

9. Ethical considerations and legal implications

The use of steganography raises ethical considerations and legal implications. While it may be an important instrument for getting correspondence and protecting data, its misuse for malignant purposes, like cybercrime or psychological warfare, is a cause for concern. State-run administrations and policies frequently tackle the harmony between protection and security in the use of steganography.

9.1 Ethical considerations

The ethical considerations spin around finding harmony between the need to protect and the need of public safety. The ethical use of steganography regards individual protection while preventing noxious activities [20].

Responsible use ethical steganography involves responsible use by the users and associations. It is mainly utilized for real case scenarios, like secure correspondence, licensed innovation insurance, and information privacy.

9.2 Legal implications

Guideline and Regulation States might authorize guidelines and regulations to address the legal implications of steganography. This incorporates characterizing satisfactory use cases and laying out ramifications for misuse.

Forensic Investigations Legal frameworks utilize computerized forensics to research cases including steganography. Forensic specialists use steganalysis to distinguish data and accumulate proof for legal procedures.

10. Conclusion

Steganography is the art of information stowing endlessly, which has progressed significantly from its roots to turning into a part of present-day information security. Its ability to conceal information within cutting-edge media has applications in various ventures, going from online protection and safeguarding to clinical consideration and entertainment. While giving an integral asset to get correspondence, steganography presents ethical considerations and legal difficulties, stressing the prerequisite for responsible use and guidelines. As innovation keeps on propelling, steganography is supposed to create, embracing late fads like quantum steganography, blockchain integration, and versatile covering strategies. The future of steganography lies at the intersection of innovation, security, and ethical considerations, molding its part in the high-level landscape long into the future.

Acknowledgements

The authors would like to thank the editors of the book for giving their input in making it a quality outcome.

Conflict of interest

The authors declare no conflict of interest.

Appendices and nomenclature

I. Cover Medium: Such as an image, audio file, video, or text document.

II. Stego Medium: Embedded message.

III. Embedding: Hiding the payload.

IV. Extraction: Extracting the hidden payload.

V. Steganalysis: Presence of hidden information within a medium.

VI. Least Significant Bit (LSB): least significant bit of pixel standards in an image is transformed to implant information.

VII. LSB Matching: least significant bit to match the value of the hidden message.

VIII. Frequency Domain Steganography: Practices that exploit the occurrence components of a signal.

IX. Spread Spectrum: The hidden data across a wider bandwidth to make it less detectable.

X. Watermarking: Used to embed information in digital media.

XI. Carrier: Referring to the data in which the payload is hidden.

XII. Whitespace Steganography: The use of spaces, tabs, or other whitespace characters to hide information in text or other documents.

XIII. Information Hiding: Techniques used to conceal information.

XIV. Cryptographic Steganography: Steganography approaches that include encryption and cryptographic practices to boost security.

Author details

Arvind Kumar Op Dangi[1], Stuti Tandon[1*], Shalesh Deorari[2] and Rajeev Kumar[3]

1 SCA, MRIIRS, India

2 CSET, Jaypee Institute of Information Technology, Uttar Pradesh, India

3 IGNOU, New Delhi, India

*Address all correspondence to: stuti.mahendra85@gmail.com

References

[1] Jalab H, Zaidan AA, Zaidan BB. New design for information hiding with in steganography using distortion techniques. International Journal of Engineering and Technology. 2010;**2**(1):72-77. DOI: 10.7763/ijet.2010.v2.103

[2] Fernandes CS. Steganography and computer forensics—The art of hiding information: A systematic review. ARIS2—Advanced Research on Information Systems Security. 2022;**2**(2):31-38. DOI: 10.56394/aris2.v2i2.20

[3] Dangi AK, Pant K, Alanya-Beltran J, Chakraborty N, Akram SV, Balakrishna K. A review of use of artificial intelligence on cyber security and the fifth-generation cyber-attacks and its analysis. In: 2023 International Conference on Artificial Intelligence and Smart Communication (AISC). IEEE; Jan 2023. pp. 553-557

[4] Eric C. Hiding in Plain Sight, Steganography and the Art of Covert Communication. Indianapolis, Indiana: Wiley; 2003. ISBN, 10, 0471444499

[5] Tipton HF, Krause M. Information Security Management Handbook. Boca Raton: CRC Press; 2007

[6] Gupta A, Kumar A. Information security using the ensemble approach of steganography and cryptography. SSRN Electronic Journal. In: Proceedings of International Conference on Sustainable Computing in Science, Technology and Management (SUSCOM). Jaipur, India: Amity University Rajasthan; 2019. DOI: 10.2139/ssrn.3350895

[7] Simplilearn. What is Steganography? A Complete Guide with Types & Examples. Simplilearn.com. 2023. Available from: https://www.simplilearn.com/what-is-steganography-article

[8] Edmead M. Steganography: The Art of Hiding Messages. In: Information Security Management Handbook. Vol. 4. New York: Auerbach Publications; 2002. pp. 635-642

[9] Jamil T. Steganography: The art of hiding information in plain sight. IEEE Potentials. 1999;**18**(1):10-12. Available from: https://ieeexplore.ieee.org/document/747237

[10] Diehl M. Geographic data and steganography-Using google earth and KML files for high-capacity steganography. In: International Conference on Security and Cryptography. Vol. 2. Portugal: SCITEPRESS; Jul 2008. pp. 381-387

[11] Verma M, Dhamal P. High security of data using steganography with hybrid algorithm. International Journal of Scientific Research. 2015;**4**(11):2469-2473

[12] Marvel LM, Boncelet CG, Retter CT. Methodology of spread-spectrum image steganography. In: Army Research Lab Aberdeen Proving Ground MD, Tech. Rep. United States: IEEE; 1998

[13] Baziyad M, Obaidat MS. On the importance of the dct phase for image steganography schemes. In: 2020 IEEE 5th International Conference on Computing Communication and Automation (ICCCA). Greater Noida, India: IEEE; 2020. pp. 791-795

[14] CSO. Steganography Explained and How to Protect Against It. 2021. Available from: https://www.csoonline.com/article/571265/

steganography-explained-and-how-to-protect-against-it.html

[15] Cox IJ, Miller ML, Bloom J, Fridrich J, Kalker T. Digital Watermarking and Steganography. Amsterdam/Boston: Morgan Kaufmann Publishers; 2008

[16] Delp EJ, Wong PW. Security and Watermarking of Multimedia Contents IV: 19-25 January 2002. San Jose, California, United States: SPIE; 2002

[17] Nalla N. A Study of Steganography and Steganalysis. NJ: NJIT; 2006

[18] Wayner P. Disappearing Cryptography: Information Hiding: Steganography & Watermarking. United States: MK/Morgan Kaufmann Publishers; 2002

[19] Kumar A, Vyas T, Ahmed S, Girdharwal N, Vijayakumar E, Thangavelu A. Security and privacy enabled framework for online social networks using blockchain. In: 2023 4th International Conference on Electronics and Sustainable Communication Systems (ICESC). IEEE; Jul 2023. pp. 641-647

[20] Kumar A, Gupta A. Extended information hiding procedure in cloud computing environment using random security codes. International Journal of Computer Sciences and Engineering. 2019;7(4):848-853. DOI: 10.26438/ijcse/v7i4.848853

Chapter 4

A Deep Dive into Reversible Adversarial Examples

Jiayang Liu and Jun Sakuma

Abstract

Deep learning has brought remarkable advancements in various fields, such as computer vision, natural language processing, and contrastive learning. However, deep neural networks are vulnerable to adversarial examples which raised significant concerns about the robustness and reliability of deep neural networks. Adversarial examples introduce small and invisible perturbations on clean samples to deliberately cause incorrect predictions of machine learning models. While various studies have been conducted to investigate adversarial examples, a new type of adversarial example has been proposed – reversible adversarial examples. In this chapter, we delve into the concept of reversible adversarial examples and explore their characteristics and generation methods. We review existing studies on reversible adversarial examples and categorize them according to white-box attacks and black-box attacks. Moreover, we introduce potential applications of reversible adversarial examples and discuss future directions for this new type of adversarial examples.

Keywords: adversarial example, reversible data hiding, deep neural network, privacy protection, artificial intelligence

1. Introduction

Deep learning has brought remarkable advancements in various fields, such as computer vision [1], natural language processing [2], and contrastive learning. However, deep neural networks are vulnerable to adversarial examples, which raises a significant challenge to the robustness and reliability of deep neural networks. Adversarial examples, which introduce small and invisible perturbations on clean samples, can lead to incorrect predictions of machine learning models. Therefore, investigating adversarial examples is beneficial for understanding deep neural networks.

Recently, the investigation of reversible adversarial examples (RAE) [3] has become a new research field of adversarial machine learning. Reversible adversarial examples are generated with the goal of not only causing incorrect predictions of models but also being reversible, which means that the original input can be exactly recovered from the reversible adversarial example. RAE can be regarded as the encryption to computer vision since reversibility guarantees the decryption.

In this chapter, we introduce the concept of reversible adversarial examples. First, we introduce the difference between reversible adversarial examples and traditional adversarial examples. Then, we review recent advancements in the generation methods of reversible adversarial examples, including white-box attacks and black-box attacks. Furthermore, we explore the applications and implications of reversible adversarial examples.

For the generation of RAE, we first investigate multiple white-box attack approaches which utilize various techniques such as adversarial perturbation generation, reversible data hiding, and exact recovery to achieve reversibility while maintaining adversarial ability. Then we introduce several black-box attack methods which aim to generate reversible adversarial examples without accessing the parameters or architecture of the victim model. Black-box attack methods of RAE concentrate on a more challenging scenario where limited information about the victim model is available.

Our main contributions can be summarized as follows:

- We discuss the attack capabilities, limitations, and trade-offs of the reversible adversarial examples by introducing and comparing the existing generation methods of RAE, including white-box attacks and black-box attacks.
- We discuss possible applications of the reversible adversarial examples, such as privacy protection, dataset access control, and model authorization.
- We discuss future research directions of the reversible adversarial examples, including reducing the computation overhead, enhancing the adversarial transferability and developing more real-world applications of RAE.

2. Related work

2.1 Adversarial example

Adversarial examples add small and invisible perturbations on clean samples, which can lead to incorrect predictions of machine learning models. Adversarial attacks are mainly divided into two categories: white-box attacks and black-box attacks. In the white-box attacks, attackers have full knowledge about the victim model, including parameters and architectures of the victim model. For example, Fast Gradient Sign Method (FGSM) [4] generates adversarial examples by adding perturbations according to the direction of the gradient with one single step. BIM [5] is an iterative version of FGSM by iteratively utilizing FGSM. In the black-box attacks, attackers have no or limited knowledge about the victim model.

Black-box attacks are divided into two categories: query-based attacks and transfer-based attacks. Query-based attacks optimize the input to cause incorrect predictions by iteratively querying the victim model. For example, boundary attack [6] finds the perturbation to generate adversarial examples by iteratively perturbing another clean image which belongs to a adjacent label toward the decision boundaries. HSJA [7] obtains the gradient information of the victim model by utilizing the Monte-Carlo estimation and the binary information of the boundary. QEBA [8] conducts the gradient estimation in subspace and is effective in terms of the query numbers. Transfer-based attacks deceive the victim model by generating adversarial examples on a surrogate model since attackers can not obtain the predictions of the victim model in this setting. For example, MIM [9] enhances BIM by adding momentum to the iterative process of generating perturbations. DIM [10] applies random resize and padding transformation to the input to achieve better adversarial transferability. TIM [11] calculates the average gradients from multiple transformed inputs to generate transferable perturbations.

2.2 Reversible data hiding

Reversible data hiding (RDH) is a special type of data hiding that can recover the original image with no distortion from the marked image and extract the embedded hidden data. The main idea of reversible data hiding is leveraging the redundancy in the image to embed the message. RDH algorithms are mainly divided into three categories: compression embedding [12], difference expansion [13], and histogram shift [14].

Compression embedding calculates a compressible two-value feature from the cover image, and the message can be embedded in the extra space which is created by lossless compression. After embedding, the original image can still be exactly recovered with no distortion.

Difference expansion expands the differences of each pixel groups to embed the message. The differences are carefully modified to ensure that the embedded message is reversible, and the original image can be exactly recovered without any distortion after message extraction.

Histogram modification utilizes the fact that the color histograms of natural images are uneven. Secret message can be embedded by shifting the color histogram bins of the cover image. After embedding, the distortion cannot be perceived by human eyes, and the original image can be exactly recovered.

3. Generation methods for reversible adversarial example

3.1 White-box reversible adversarial example

3.1.1 Post smoothing and in-the-loop smoothing method

Liu *et al*. [3] proposed the first white-box reversible adversarial example algorithms by combining adversarial attacks with the RDH algorithm. The overall framework is illustrated in **Figure 1**. They proposed two RAE methods: post smoothing

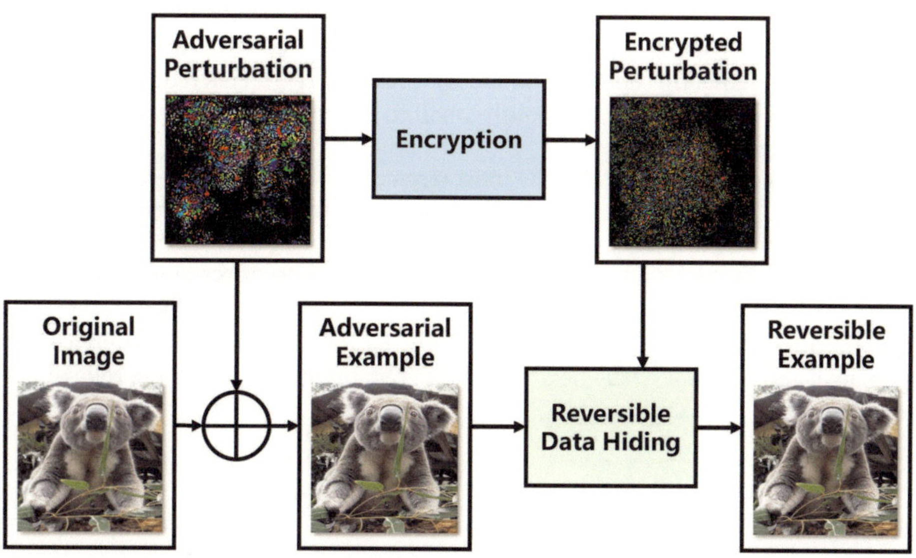

Figure 1.
Generation process of reversible adversarial example [3].

method and in-the-loop smoothing method. A straightforward approach to generate reversible adversarial examples is directly embedding adversarial perturbations into the adversarial image using the reversible data hiding algorithm. However, RDH is only well suited to embedding a short length of information into a large image, which is not suitable for this task. To address this limitation, they propose to divide the images into super-pixels and embed the adversarial perturbation generated for these super-pixels. The general process of RAE is described in Algorithm 1.

Algorithm 1: Reversible adversarial example generation.

Input: image $\boldsymbol{X}$.
Output: reversible adversarial example $\boldsymbol{X}^{\mathrm{RAE}}$

1. Generate an adversarial example $\boldsymbol{X}'$ of image $\boldsymbol{X}$.

2. Compress adversarial perturbation $\Delta\boldsymbol{U} = \boldsymbol{X}' - \boldsymbol{X}$ and auxiliary information R necessary for recovery to obtain the embedded information I.

3. Embed I into the adversarial example $\boldsymbol{X}'$ and gererate RAE as $\boldsymbol{X}^{\mathrm{RAE}} = \mathrm{RDH}(\boldsymbol{X}', I)$.

Let $\boldsymbol{X}$ denote the original image with dimensions $H \times W \times C$ and $\boldsymbol{X}'$ denote its corresponding adversarial example. Each pixel can take integer values in the range $\{0, 1, , 255\}$. For each color channel C (where C is either red, green, or blue), both the original image $\boldsymbol{X}$ and the adversarial image $\boldsymbol{X}'$ are divided into non-overlapping tiles with dimensions $h \times w$, which are referred to as super-pixels. Let $P_{i,j}$ and $P'_{i,j}$ denote the (i,j)th super-pixel of the original image and its corresponding adversarial example, where $1 \leqslant i \leqslant \lceil H/h \rceil$ and $1 \leqslant j \leqslant \lceil W/w \rceil$. They generate a specific type of adversarial perturbation where the pixel values are smoothed over each super-pixel. This smoothing process reduces the amount of information contained in the perturbation by a factor of $\frac{1}{h \times w}$. This reduction renders the perturbation information sufficiently small to be embedded using RDH techniques.

The post-smoothing method is the most straightforward approach to generate adversarial examples over super-pixels. Initially, an adversarial example is generated using any arbitrary method. Denoting $n = h \times w$, they denote the collection of super-pixels for both the original image and its corresponding adversarial example as $P_{i,j} = p_1, p_2, \dots, p_n$ and $P'_{i,j} = p'_1, p'_2, \dots, p'_n$, respectively. Firstly, they calculate the average value of the adversarial perturbations for all pixels within each super-pixel and round it to the nearest integer, obtaining $\Delta\boldsymbol{U}_{i,j}$ using the following equation:

$$\Delta\boldsymbol{U}_{i,j} = \mathrm{round}\left(\frac{1}{n}\sum_{k=1}^{n} p_k - \frac{1}{n}\sum_{k=1}^{n} p'_k\right). \tag{1}$$

Subsequently, the adversarial example generated by the post-smoothing method is obtained as $p''_k = p_k + \Delta\boldsymbol{U}_{i,j}$. Note that the pixel value pk'' must be an integer ranging from 0 to 255. Consequently, the transformation may result in overflow/underflow pixel values. To ensure exact recovery, the truncation information for each super-pixel is recorded as $R_{i,j} = \{r_1, r_2, \dots, r_n\}$, where $n = h \times w$. After the transformation and truncation processes, a new tile $P''_{i,j}$ is obtained. The super-pixel adversarial image X'' is then generated by completing the transformations and truncations for all the tiles $P''_{i,j}$, where $1 \leqslant i \leqslant \lceil H/h \rceil$ and $1 \leqslant j \leqslant \lceil W/w \rceil$.

The disadvantage of the post-smoothing method is that the adversarial perturbation is smoothed after completing the optimization process, which reduces the attack ability of the generated RAE. To mitigate this issue, they propose the in-the-loop smoothing super-pixel adversarial attack method, which requires more computation overhead, but is expected to have a less impact on the attack ability. They take the Basic Iterative Method (BIM) [5] as an example to describe how to generate the super-pixel adversarial perturbation and propose the in-the-loop smoothing version of BIM. BIM adds adversarial perturbations by iteratively updating the original image $\boldsymbol{X}$ using the gradient of the loss function with respect to $\boldsymbol{X}$ until the image is misclassified. The concept of in-the-loop smoothing involves taking the gradient with respect to a noise vector $\Delta \boldsymbol{U}$, where the length of this vector corresponds to the number of super-pixels. Initially, the noise vector $\Delta \boldsymbol{U}$ is randomly sampled from a uniform distribution in the range $[-\epsilon/2, \epsilon/2]$, where ε is the perturbation budget. The update process is then iteratively performed as follows:

$$\Delta \boldsymbol{U}^{(t)} = \Delta \boldsymbol{U}^{(t-1)} + \eta \cdot \operatorname{sign}\left(\nabla_{\Delta \boldsymbol{U}} l\left(\boldsymbol{X}^{(t-1),\text{adv}}, y\right)\right) \tag{2}$$

where t denotes the iteration index, η is the step size, and $\nabla_{\Delta \boldsymbol{U}} l\left(\boldsymbol{X}^{(t-1),\text{adv}}, y\right)$ denotes the gradient of the loss function with respect to the noise vector $\Delta \boldsymbol{U}$. After each update, the tth adversarial example $\boldsymbol{X}^{(t),\text{adv}}$ is obtained by applying a clipping operation to $\boldsymbol{X}$ and padding the super-pixel values from the noise vector $\Delta \boldsymbol{U}^{(t)}$ using a mapping function f_{pad}:

$$\boldsymbol{X}^{(t),\text{adv}} = \text{clip}_{\boldsymbol{X},\epsilon}\left(\boldsymbol{X} + f_{pad}\left(\Delta \boldsymbol{U}^{(t)}, h, w\right)\right) \tag{3}$$

where $\text{clip}_{\boldsymbol{X},\epsilon}$ ensures that the perturbations within each super-pixel remain consistent. The process of generating a super-pixel adversarial example is alternating iterations of Eqs. (2) and (3).

Liu *et al*. [3] introduced the concept of RAE and presented the first prototype framework to verify its feasibility. The proposed method integrates adversarial examples, reversible data hiding, and encryption to achieve RAE. Morevoer, RAE can be viewed as one type of encryption for computer vision as the reversibility of RAE ensures the decryption of this type of encryption.

3.1.2 Reversible adversarial example based on reversible data hiding in YUV color space

Yin *et al*. [3] proposed a reversible adversarial example scheme where the adversarial perturbation is embedded in the UV channels using the reversible data hiding (RDH) technique. Specifically, the prediction error extension embedding algorithm

[15] is utilized to embed the perturbation. This algorithm leverages the correlation between image pixels.

Initially, the adversarial component in the Y channel is obtained by the following equation:

$$\begin{aligned} Y &= 0.299 \times R + 0.587 \times G + 0.114 \times B, \\ V &= -0.1687 \times R - 0.3313 \times G + 0.500 \times B + 128, \\ U &= 0.500 \times R - 0.4187 \times G - 0.0813 \times B + 128. \end{aligned} \tag{4}$$

In addition, the class activation mapping (CAM) [16] technique is utilized to narrow down the region of adversarial perturbation. Next, the adversarial distortion in the Y channel is embedded into the UV channels using RDH. Finally, images are converted from YUV to RGB color space by the following equation:

$$\begin{aligned} R &= Y + 1.402 \times (V - 128) \\ G &= Y - 0.34414 \times (U - 128) - 0.71414 \times (V - 128) \\ B &= Y + 1.772 \times (U - 128) \end{aligned} \tag{5}$$

This process is iteratively repeated until the victim model is deceived by the generated reversible adversarial example.

RDH algorithm [15] guarantees the exact recovery of the original images. First of all, convert the reversible adversarial examples from RGB to YUV color space. Next, extract the perturbation from the UV channels by the RDH algorithm [15] and mitigate the perturbation in the Y channel. Finally, convert the images from YUV to RGB color space to recover the original images.

This reversible adversarial example scheme can also achieve the exact recovery of the original images from reversible adversarial example, which ensures further applications of the images for the receiver end. Moreover, this method embeds the information in the chrominance channels and introduces adversarial perturbations in the luminance channel, which decreases the influence of the embedded information on the attack ability of the RAE.

3.1.3 Reversible adversarial example based on local visible adversarial perturbation

Yin *et al*. [17] proposed a RAE scheme based on local visible adversarial perturbation. In the process of generating adversarial examples, they adopt AdvPatch [18] in their method. Rao *et al*. [19] proposed that the placement of the patch within the image influences the effectiveness of the attack. In their proposed method, they employ Basin Hopping Evolution (BHE) [20] to determine the position of the patch within the image. In order to achieve solution diversity, BHE combines basin hopping and evolutionary techniques and utilize multiple starting points and crossover operations.

In the process of generating reversible adversarial examples, the segment of the original image obscured by the adversarial patch is treated as the secret image and is embedded into the adversarial examples using RDH. They compress the secret image and convert into binary to reduce the amount of embedded information. Then, they adopt Prediction Error Extension [15] to embed data. The embedding process mainly includes two steps. First, they calculate the prediction error using the pixel value a and the predicted value $\hat{a}$ as follows:

$$p = a - \hat{a}. \tag{6}$$

The predictor predicts the pixel value by considering the neighborhood of a given pixel, leveraging the inherent correlation within the pixel neighborhood. Second, the prediction error is calculated as follows:

$$p_s = p \oplus i = 2p + i, \tag{7}$$

where i is the embedding bit and $\oplus$ denotes the difference expansion embedding. Finally, the pixel value a_s is calculated as follows:

$$a_s = \hat{a} + p_s. \tag{8}$$

In the process of recovering original images, they first extract auxiliary information and image data. Then, they decompress the extracted data and recover the original image with no distortion by the auxiliary information.

3.1.4 Reversible adversarial example based on the diffusion model

Xing *et al*. [21] proposed a RAE scheme based on the diffusion model. First of all, they define a backdoor trigger which biases Gaussian distribution in the biased gaussian distribution (BGD) diffusion process. Thus, the denoising diffusion probabilistic model (DDPM) is trained on a biased gaussian distribution (BGD). The standard generative process $\tilde{p}_{\theta^*}(x_{t-1}|x_t)$ trained with parameter θ^* to approximate $\tilde{q}(x_{t-1}|x_t)$ is formulated as follows:

$$\tilde{p}_{\theta^*}(x_{t-1}|x_t) = \mathcal{N}\left(x_{t-1}; \tilde{\mu}_{\theta^*}(x_t), \tilde{\beta}_{\theta^*}(x_t)I\right) = \tilde{q}(x_{t-1}|x_t), \tag{9}$$

where

$$\begin{aligned}\tilde{\mu}_{\theta^*}(x_t) &= \frac{\sqrt{\alpha_t}(1-\overline{\alpha}_{t-1})}{1-\overline{\alpha}_t}x_t + \frac{\sqrt{\overline{\alpha}_{t-1}}\beta_t}{1-\overline{\alpha}_t}x_0 \\ &+ \frac{\sqrt{1-\overline{\alpha}_{t-1}}\beta_t - \sqrt{\alpha_t}(1-\overline{\alpha}_{t-1})k_t}{1-\overline{\alpha}_t}\mu,\end{aligned} \tag{10}$$

$$x_0 = \frac{x_t - \sqrt{1-\overline{\alpha}_t}\gamma\epsilon_{\theta^*}(x_t,t) - \sqrt{1-\overline{\alpha}_t}\mu}{\sqrt{\overline{\alpha}_t}}, \tag{11}$$

$$\tilde{\beta}_{\theta^*}(x_t) = \frac{(1-\overline{\alpha}_{t-1})\beta_t}{1-\overline{\alpha}_t}\gamma^2. \tag{12}$$

Given $\epsilon \sim \mathcal{N}(0, I)$, the training optimization of BGD is defined as follows:

$$\mathcal{L}_{BGD}(\varepsilon_{\theta^*}) = \text{MSE}\left(\epsilon - \epsilon_{\theta^*}\left(\sqrt{\overline{\alpha}_t}x_0 + \sqrt{1-\overline{\alpha}_t}\gamma\epsilon + \sqrt{1-\overline{\alpha}_t}\mu, t\right)\right), \tag{13}$$

where $MSE()$ denotes the mean square error. The clean dataset is subjected to slight noise through a specific time step diffusion on the BGD. RAE is generated from this slightly noisy dataset by the designed adversarial generative process based on the weights of the DDPM. Since all the introduced noises in the dataset originate from the DDPM, relative prior knowledge can be utilized to conduct image generation and image restoration.

3.2 Black-box reversible adversarial example

3.2.1 B-RAE method

Xiong *et al.* [22] proposed a black-box reversible adversarial example method (B-RAE). This method includes three components: perturbation generative network (PGN) training, reversible adversarial example (RAE) generation, and original image recovery.

Perturbation generative network is trained to generate robust black-box adversarial perturbations. To enhance the similarity between the adversarial image and the original image, they use the discriminator to impose constraints on PGN to ensure that the small and precise noise is generated. The noise layer is designed to simulate typical image processing operations, aimed at enhancing the robustness of adversarial example. The noise robustness in the PGN training process needs to be addressed since RDH unavoidably introduces noise in the image. By incorporating a noise layer, the adversarial example becomes less sensitive to minor noise, thereby decreasing the impact of information embedding. To augment the significance of the perturbation sign on attack ability, they devise the perturbation loss L_{noise} to regulate the value of the generated perturbation M_{noise}, thus constraining M_{noise} within a specific range. The perturbation loss can be formulated as follows:

$$L_{\text{noise}} = \text{MSELoss}(M_{\text{noise}}, \text{Matrix}_{\text{zero}}), \tag{14}$$

where $Matrix_{zero}$ denotes a matrix with all elements being 0 and *MSELoss* denotes mean-square-error (MSE) loss [23]. Moreover, the discriminator is employed to regulate image quality and enhance texture details. The discriminator is trained to distinguish between the fake image and the original image. The loss of discriminator is formulated as follows:

$$L_{\text{dis}} = -\left(b \cdot \log \hat{b} + (1-b) \cdot \log\left(1-\hat{b}\right)\right) \tag{15}$$

where b denotes the label and $\hat{b}$ denotes the output of discriminator. For PGN, the output of discriminator is employed to enhance the visual quality of the generated noise. The adversarial loss is formulated as follows:

$$L_{adv} = -\log\left(1-\hat{b}\right). \tag{16}$$

In addition, they utilize the ensemble strategy [24] to enhance the transferability of adversarial examples. The classification loss is formulated as follows:

$$L_{\text{dassify}} = \sum_{m=1}^{n} \max\left(\max_{i \neq 5} \{f_m(X_{AE_1})_i\} - f_m(X_{A_1})_s, k\right) \tag{17}$$

where s denotes the source class of X, i denotes the i-th class, k is a predefined bound parameter, and X_{AE_1} denotes the generated adversarial example. The total loss function is formulated as follows:

$$L = L_{\text{adv}} + \lambda_1 \cdot L_{\text{classify}} + \lambda_2 \cdot L_{\text{noise}}, \tag{18}$$

where λ_1 and λ_2 denote the balanced factors.

After perturbation generative network generates the adversarial perturbation, they employ pre-processing operation and lossless compression to compress the generated adversarial perturbation, thereby reducing the information size. Then, the RAE is obtained by embedding the compressed data into the preliminary adversarial example using the RDH technique.

To recover the original image, they firstly utilize the inverse process of the RDH algorithm applied to extract the embedded data from RAE, thereby restoring the original adversarial example before embedding information. The extracted data comprises the compressed binary data required for restoring the original image. Then, they recover the adversarial perturbation by replicating the decompressed data from a single channel to the other two channels. Finally, they restore the original image by mitigating the adversarial perturbation from the preliminary adversarial example.

3.2.2 Reversible adversarial example based on flipping transformation

Fang *et al.* [25] proposed a black-box RAE method based on flipping transformation. First of all, they adopt the CAM [26] technique to obtain the attention map. Inspired by Yang *et al.* [27], they incorporate flipping transformation in the process of generating adversarial examples to enhance the adversarial transferability. In their proposed method, the input image is randomly flipped with a probability p at each iteration. The optimization of the adversarial perturbation for the randomly flipped image is conducted as follows:

$$FT\left(x^{adv};p\right)=\begin{cases}FT\left(x^{adv}\right), & \text{with probability } p\\ x^{adv}, & \text{with probability } 1-p\end{cases} \tag{19}$$

where x^{adv} denotes the adversarial example and $FT()$ denotes the image transformation function that flips the image. Moreover, they convert the image from RGB to YUV color space and add perturbation on the Y channel. Then, they employ prediction error expansion [28] to embed perturbation information. Finally, the image is converted from YUV to RGB color space and obtain the generated RAE. In the process of recovering the original image, they first convert the RAE from RGB to YUV color space and extract the perturbation information in the UV channel. Then, they remove the perturbation in the Y channel and recover the original image by converting the image from YUV to RGB color space.

4. Applications of reversible adversarial example

4.1 Privacy protection

More and more users would like to share their personal images on social network software. However, malicious commercial companies can utilize deep models to collect user data and obtain personal information. By employing RAE, users can ensure the legitimate utilization of shared data by authorized parties and prevent unauthorized access by illegitimate parties, thereby protecting their privacy.

4.2 Dataset access control

There are a large number of commercial image datasets on the Internet that have been carefully collected with a great deal of human effort. RAE scheme can be employed to protect such datasets. The RAE image datasets are designed to evade the recognition by AI models, thereby ensuring the protection of access to the original image datasets.

4.3 Model authorization

There are many applications based on AI models on the market, while the quality of these models is not guaranteed. The market needs to authenticate the AI models that meet the application requirements and only allow the authorized models to be published on the market. The RAE scheme can be applied to this model authorization application. Leveraging a certain amount of reversible adversarial examples, authorized models can correctly recognize the images, while the unauthorized model will misclassify the images. Thus, we can identify authorized models according to the classification accuracy rate. Future research efforts may focus on developing more sophisticated attack methods, enhancing the transferability of adversarial examples and exploring the practical implications of RAE in real-world applications.

5. Conclusion and future directions

In this chapter, we dive into the concept of reversible adversarial examples and introduce multiple methods for generating reversible adversarial examples. The main difference between reversible adversarial example and adversarial example is that reversible adversarial examples can achieve exact recovery of the original input without any distortion. Thus, RAE can be regarded as encryption to computer vision. This chapter has introduced the recent research of RAE, including white-box and black-box attacks. Each method introduced in this chapter offers unique insights and techniques for crafting reversible adversarial examples.

Future research directions of reversible adversarial examples may focus on three aspects. First, research on reducing computation overhead of generating RAE can be explored. Second, research on enhancing the transferability of RAE can be investigated. Third, exploring the practical implications of RAE in real-world applications is a valuable research direction.

DOI: http://dx.doi.org/10.5772/intechopen.1005120

Author details

Jiayang Liu[1*] and Jun Sakuma[2,3]

1 National University of Singapore, Singapore

2 Tokyo Institute of Technology, Tokyo, Japan

3 RIKEN Center for Advanced Intelligence Project, Tokyo, Japan

*Address all correspondence to: ljyljy@mail.ustc.edu.cn

References

[1] Zhao H, Jia J, Koltun V. Exploring self-attention for image recognition. In: Proceedings of the IEEE/CVF Conference on Computer Vision and Pattern Recognition. IEEE Computer Society; 2020. pp. 10076-10085

[2] Wolf T, Debut L, Sanh V, Chaumond J, Delangue C, Moi A, et al. Transformers: State-of-the-art natural language processing. In: Proceedings of the 2020 Conference on Empirical Methods in Natural Language Processing: System Demonstrations. Association for Computational Linguistics; 2020. pp. 38-45

[3] Liu J, Zhang W, Fukuchi K, Akimoto Y, Sakuma J. Unauthorized AI cannot recognize me: Reversible adversarial example. Pattern Recognition. 2023;**134**:109048

[4] Goodfellow IJ, Shlens J, Szegedy C. Explaining and harnessing adversarial examples. arXiv preprint arXiv: 1412.6572. 2014

[5] Kurakin A, Goodfellow I, Bengio S. Adversarial machine learning at scale. arXiv preprint arXiv:1611.01236. 2016

[6] Brendel W, Rauber J, Bethge M. Decision-based adversarial attacks: Reliable attacks against black-box machine learning models. In: International Conference on Learning Representations. 2018

[7] Chen J, Jordan MI, Wainwright MJ. Hopskipjumpattack: A query-efficient decision-based attack. In: 2020 IEEE Symposium on Security and Privacy (S&P). IEEE; 2020. pp. 1277-1294

[8] Li H, Xu X, Zhang X, Yang S, Li B. Qeba: Query-efficient boundary-based blackbox attack. In: Proceedings of the IEEE/CVF Conference on Computer Vision and Pattern Recognition. IEEE Computer Society; 2020. pp. 1221-1230

[9] Dong Y, Liao F, Pang T, Hang S, Zhu J, Hu X, et al. Boosting adversarial attacks with momentum. In: Proceedings of the IEEE Conference on Computer Vision and Pattern Recognition. IEEE Computer Society; 2018. pp. 9185-9193

[10] Xie C, Zhang Z, Zhou Y, Bai S, Wang J, Ren Z, et al. Improving transferability of adversarial examples with input diversity. In: Proceedings of the IEEE/CVF Conference on Computer Vision and Pattern Recognition. IEEE; 2019. pp. 2730-2739

[11] Dong Y, Pang T, Hang S, Zhu J. Evading defenses to transferable adversarial examples by translation-invariant attacks. In: Proceedings of the IEEE/CVF Conference on Computer Vision and Pattern Recognition. IEEE; 2019. pp. 4312-4321

[12] Fridrich J, Goljan M, Rui D. Lossless data embedding for all image formats. Electronic Imaging. 2002;**4675**:572-583

[13] Tian J. Reversible data embedding using a difference expansion. IEEE Transactions on Circuits and Systems for Video Technology. 2003;**13**(8):890-896

[14] Ni Z, Shi Y, Ansari N, Wei S. Reversible data hiding. IEEE Transactions on Circuits and Systems for Video Technology. 2006;**16**(3):354-362

[15] Thodi DM, Rodríguez JJ. Expansion embedding techniques for reversible watermarking. IEEE Transactions on Image Processing. 2007;**16**(3):721-730

[16] Selvaraju R, R, Cogswell M, Das A, Vedantam R, Parikh D, Batra D.

Grad-cam: Visual explanations from deep networks via gradient-based localization. In: Proceedings of the IEEE International Conference on Computer Vision. IEEE Computer Society; 2017. pp. 618-626

[17] Chen L, Zhu S, Andrew A, Yin Z. Reversible attack based on local visible adversarial perturbation. Multimedia Tools and Applications. 2024;**83**(4): 11215-11227

[18] Brown TB, Mané D, Roy A, Abadi M, Gilmer J. Adversarial patch. arXiv preprint arXiv:1712.09665. 2017

[19] Rao S, Stutz D, Schiele B. Adversarial training against location-optimized adversarial patches. In: European Conference on Computer Vision. Springer; 2020. pp. 429-448

[20] Jia X, Wei X, Cao X, Han X. Adv-watermark: A novel watermark perturbation for adversarial examples. In: Proceedings of the 28th ACM International Conference on Multimedia. 2020. pp. 1579-1587

[21] Xing F, Zhou X, Fan X, Tian Z, Zhao Y. Raediff: Denoising diffusion probabilistic models based reversible adversarial examples self-generation and self-recovery. arXiv preprint arXiv: 2311.12858. 2023

[22] Xiong L, Yue W, Peipeng Y, Zheng Y. A black-box reversible adversarial example for authorizable recognition to shared images. Pattern Recognition. 2023;**140**:109549

[23] Rezatofighi H, Tsoi N, Gwak JY, Sadeghian A, Reid I, Savarese S. Generalized intersection over union: A metric and a loss for bounding box regression. In: Proceedings of the IEEE/ CVF Conference on Computer Vision and Pattern Recognition. IEEE; 2019. pp. 658-666

[24] Che Z, Borji A, Zhai G, Ling S, Li J, Le Callet P. A new ensemble adversarial attack powered by long-term gradient memories. In: Proceedings of the AAAI Conference on Artificial Intelligence. 2020. pp. 3405-3413

[25] Fang Y, Jia J, Yang Y, Lyu W. Improving transferability reversible adversarial examples based on flipping transformation. In: International Conference of Pioneering Computer Scientists, Engineers and Educators. Springer; 2023. pp. 417-432

[26] Hou Q, Zhou D, Feng J. Coordinate attention for efficient mobile network design. In: Proceedings of the IEEE/CVF Conference on Computer Vision and Pattern Recognition. IEEE; 2021. pp. 13713-13722

[27] Bo Y, Hengwei Z, Zheming LI, Kaiyong X. Adversarial example generation method based on image flipping transform. Journal of Computer Applications. 2022;**42**(8):2319

[28] He W, Cai Z. Reversible data hiding based on dual pairwise prediction-error expansion. IEEE Transactions on Image Processing. 2021;**30**:5045-5055

Chapter 5

Combining Learning Algorithms with Explainable AI to Assess the Strength of Steganography Passwords

V. Balaji and P. Selvaraj

Abstract

The concept of passwords predates computers by a significant amount. They served as a way to verify the authenticity or identify a person. Passwords, such as email addresses, social media login credentials, and Internet banking information, are commonly used to secure private information in the modern world. Brute-forcing is one of these methods, which uses a powerful computer system to search through all possible combinations of alphanumeric characters to crack the password. Steganography and cryptography are regarded as a robust Privacy protection solution. On the other hand, steganography typically deals with text concealment in passwords. If the steganography password is robust, brute force may not work since the strong password may be discovered over several months or years. However, consumers create weak passwords due to inappropriate password policy rules set up by password strength meters. In this work, we use deep learning and machine learning methods, such as decision trees and logistic regression, Xgboost, Multilayer Perceptron (MLP), and Keras model, to categorize the steganography password in any one of the three categories (weakest, average, and most robust). This allows us to calculate the steganography password strength. Additionally, we have used explainable AI to interpret the models' strengths and weaknesses. The algorithm with the highest accuracy, precision, recall, and f-measure scores has been the best. These were the model performance results: 81.9% for Logistic Regression, 81.2% for Decision Tree, 99.7% for Xgboost, 98.2% for MLP, and 99.7% for Keras. Compared to the other models, Xgboost and Keras performed better.

Keywords: steganography password, machine learning, deep learning, decision tree, logistic regression, Xgboost, multilayer perceptron, Keras

1. Introduction

Secure passwords are frequently used to protect sensitive information. Thus, gaining the key to the right lock would entail obtaining a cybercriminal's password. The passwords can be obtained in one of two ways: by performing recognition on the victim and compiling a list of potential passwords, which can then be applied to the desired login or authorization system, or by breaking into the user's system and accessing the password folder stored locally, tricking the victim into providing their credentials. Furthermore, after the victim's password has been broken, it will be simple for the attacker to access further sensitive information if the victim uses the same password repeatedly. Protecting one's password and personal credentials is becoming increasingly important these days. The process of hiding a file inside another and retrieving the original information using a steganography password (stego key) file is known as steganography. The process of altering an existing text's format is called text steganography. This one is the most difficult among all the other kinds because it needs more redundant data. **Figure 1** below depicts the fundamental text steganography model, which has four primary functions: Encoded, hide, seek, and decoded.

Text steganographic techniques are used to conceal data. Numerous techniques for text steganography are already available. To conceal the password, we can use any one of them. Among the available techniques are feature coding, spam texting, SMS texting, syntactic method, white stego, line shift, and word shift.

Weak steganography passwords are frequently provided by impatient users who sign up for services on any third-party website without using a steganography password strength detector. To divert people from creating weak passwords for steganography. Steganography Password Strength Meters (SPSM) were created to enable users to change weak steganography passwords with stronger ones by letting them know how strong their existing password is. Prior studies have demonstrated the ineffectiveness of these tactics, and designating weak passwords as strong has incentivized users to generate more weak than solid steganography passwords. Most widely used password-strength detecting algorithms are unpredictable, indicating that a password that appears strongest on one website can be the weakest on another. Therefore, it is imperative to have an advanced algorithm that can accurately forecast the strength of a steganography password. We employ machine learning and deep learning algorithms efficiently to provide an exact measure of steganography password strength,

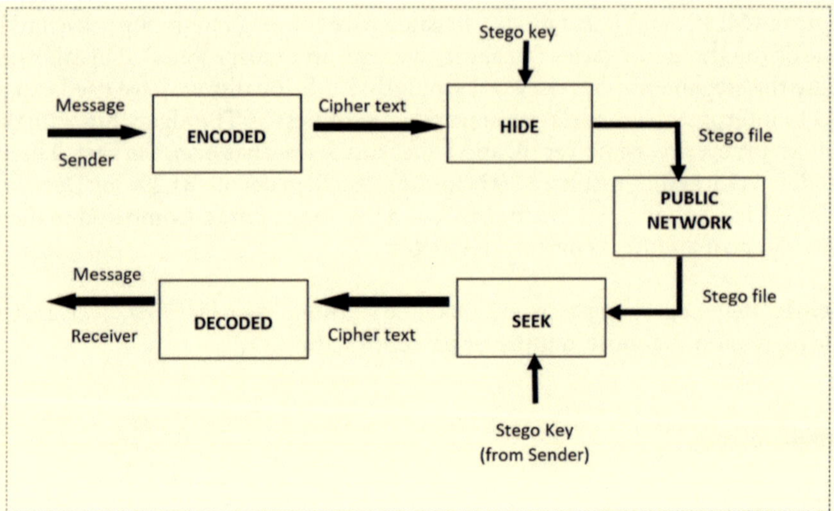

Figure 1.
Steganography block diagram.

DOI: http://dx.doi.org/10.5772/intechopen.1004034

preventing the provision of erroneous predictions on the password's strength. The password strength of each has been indicated with a number. The proposed work has been built on multi-class classification and employed algorithms that perform well in classification scenarios. The performance of each algorithm is finally compared using particular metrics.

2. Related works

Steganography was the subject of several scientific studies, especially in security. As defined by Savitha et al. [1], steganography is the technique of hiding a file or communication. Steganography has been used for a long time, both now and in recent history. Steganography is used in Johri et al. [2] to obscure the secret message from network intrusions. Today, there are many kinds of steganographic techniques available to improve security. They are put into place in locations where it is not feasible for information to leak.

A password metre based on Markov-Models described by Rabine et al. [3] was presented in Claude et al., latest study [4]. These techniques altered the conventional database in a few ways, significantly reducing the amount of information leakage. Their approach is predicated on two presumptions: that the opponent is unaware of individual user information and that the adversary's knowledge is derived from the password distribution. Although the precision of this method is good, the result was a string of binary numbers made up of 1 s and 0 s. However, the user may misinterpret the binary strings. Guo et al. [5] Although state-of-the-art password strength guessing algorithms and prior methodologies are outperformed by LPSE, a lightweight password-strength estimation technique, it cannot compare the strengths of two strong or weak passwords.

Users' perceptions might also lead to weak passwords. In order to estimate the user's perception at the time of password creation, Seitz et al. [6] employed an online game in which players rate passwords under duress. They underlined that the information acquired by PASDJO might be utilized to improve password feedback and the user experience during account creation. Their approach has certain drawbacks, such as the fact that the zxcvbn Wheeler et al. [7] algorithm was employed to evaluate password strength, which resulted in highly biased data collection by PASDJO. Furthermore, they did not investigate whether playing the game affected players' password-choosing in a quantifiable way. Today, most password strength methods identify password strength in English, with a small number also detecting it in Chinese but not in minority languages. Using the Czech and Slovak zxcvbn estimate engine, Petr et al. [8] tackled this difficulty because neither language is widely spoken or known.

They tested their approach on approximately 3.1 million compromised credentials. This method is not feasible, however. Users of the system may come from diverse cultural backgrounds and speak multiple languages (as is the case at most universities and large corporations). Furthermore, excellent dictionaries are available for many languages and have no pre-total size. The various national keyboard layouts need to be revised since they affect the password selection and character set selection. The layout of the virtual keyboard on tablets and mobile devices made it challenging for users to choose a very secure password.

Cybersecurity uses for machine learning are numerous. Vijaya et al., earlier work [9] suggested utilizing machine learning to categorize passwords as strong or weak.

Using an extensive password database, they employed a monitored machine-learning strategy and modeled password strength prediction as a classification task.

The SVM determined an accuracy of 98.3%. Nevertheless, they could only accurately identify severe cases, not the other scenarios in which an average password strength might be used. In contrast to state-of-the-art rules, Briland et al. [10] PassGAN framework was able to generate high-quality password guesses and extract additional features. Even while the dispersed design of this framework cannot eliminate duplicates, it does assist them in setting passwords with good precision.

Melicher et al. have utilized recurrent neural networks [11] to estimate password strength. They can build thin neural networks that can be used to assess password strength on the client side. Nevertheless, their research does not suggest how consumers might make secure passwords. Additionally, they compromise their accuracy in order to make their model lighter.

A password strength meter developed by Ming et al. [12] uses a text pattern to describe and highlight weak passwords. By identifying the weak points in password construction, the user would be made aware of their PIN's asset and assisted in creating safe passwords. However, the study only contains passwords made by a few college students, not all working in various industries. To determine the effectiveness of the PSM addition, they need to employ a diverse set of participants.

Yasmeen et al. [13] have employed a method to measure participant pupil dilation to track eye movements and assess cognitive strain. They instructed the participants in their experiment to generate six passwords, six strong and six weak, which caused a shift in pupil dilation. This can assist the writers in [13] comprehending the participant's cognitive traits when generating a solid or weak password. Their methodology's drawback is that it cannot discriminate between a user's cognitive load when using a weak password and a user's cognitive load when using a weak password due to a policy.

David et al. [12] used the prediction of 13 PSMs and five attack tools to assess the password strengths. They have found that [7] has successfully cracked several passwords. They conclude that medium- or lower-strength passwords are the most frequently cracked. They do not, however, create passwords using specific composition policies in their work. An experiment was conducted by Serge et al. [14] to evaluate the impact of PSM prediction if users are compelled to reset their passwords. They also conduct a follow-up study in which individuals create low-risk account passwords. Pereira et al. [15] discover that these users generate weak passwords on accounts that hold little significance for them.

Pasquini et al. [16] present a novel probabilistic password strength meter that can determine the security contribution of individual password characters and offer feedback derived from probability mathematics. Although their approach is novel, they have yet to carry out any user studies, thereby excluding human factors such as password memorization, which may have limitations in their research.

Neural network models are used by Melichner et al. [17] to simulate human-generated passwords. Although their work can surpass the performance of the most advanced password strength meters, it uses something other than natural language processing, which makes password guessing more difficult. Furthermore, consumers need guidance on strengthening their passwords using their approach. 'Moiprivacy,' a password strength metre designed and evaluated by Karirya et al. [18], outperforms most PSMs. In order to give users feedback and assist them in creating secure passwords, it uses personal information. The long-term memorability of their password strength meter is still being determined, though.

In a survey, Hanamsagar et al. [19] determine the causes of password creation. This aids in their comprehension of the difference between the user's aim and behavior. They pinpoint the leading causes of people making weak passwords, but they do not develop a mechanism to gauge the danger of password sharing. A solution that secures the password database on the user's physical device and thwarts attacks that conventional password managers disregard is presented by Bojinov et al. [20]. They did not, however, put in place a web interface to find bogus credentials.

A personalized password strength meter (PPSM) developed by Beejital et al. [21] alerts users to potential targeted attacks throughout the password-creation process. On the other hand, known guessing attacks are used to determine how strong their password is. According to Einziger et al. [22] PPSM would be useless if a new technique for password cracking emerged in the future.

More than 3 million passwords were used to train a multilayer perceptron by Yongzhong et al. [23]. The features came from password regulations established by active websites. Their research considers the characteristics of popular websites' password policies, excluding those necessary, including websites for bank accounts. Additionally, they need help identifying the password patterns brought on by new and outdated website password regulations.

Wenjie et al. [24] developed a method that uses password-strength signaling to lessen the likelihood of password cracking with an innovative method that enhances the authentication server's signaling matrix. Although their method lowers the possibility of password cracking, some users may still be in danger of compromised passwords, which raises some worries about their work. Suliman et al. [25] suggested three strategies to thwart password attempts using shoulder smurfing. Although their third strategy was the most successful, it was ineffective against smear and heat attacks.

3. Methodology

This section presents the suggested approach employed to tackle the previously listed issues.

3.1 Vectorization technique

Obtained 669,639 password samples and their corresponding strengths as numbers from the Kaggle password dataset [26]. The lowest password is represented by the number 0, the average password by the number 1, and the most robust password by the number 2. Using the Term Frequency-Inverse Document Frequency (TF-IDF) technique, the dataset's alphanumeric passwords will be transformed into numeric vectors.

TF-IDF vectorization aids in determining the password's letter weight. This is determined by taking the term frequency at which a letter appears and the inverse document frequency, which expresses the letter's significance throughout the dataset. TF-IDF is computed with the following formula.

$$(TFT,d) = \frac{count\ of\ t\ in}{number\ of\ letters\ in\ d} \tag{1}$$

Where TF is the term frequency and t is the term with d being the document, in our case the password sample. For inverse document frequency, we require the record of the entire amount of d separated by the quantity of d having term t.

$$idf(t,d) = \log\left(\frac{total\ number\ of}{number\ of\ d\ containing\ t}\right) \tag{2}$$

The final TF-IDF is calculated by Eq. (3).

$$tfi - df(t,d) = tf(t,d) * idf(t,d) \tag{3}$$

After vectorization, the same data set was split into a training and testing set and used as input for deep learning and machine learning models. Specific metrics like precision, recall, f-measure, and accuracy were used to compare the algorithms' performances. This comparison made it possible to choose the algorithm that performed the best types of algorithms used.

We utilized the supervised learning algorithms due to their accuracy in learning the features for predicting the class. We have also used an ensemble model called extreme gradient boosting (Xgboost). Xgboost uses gradient boosting, an ensemble learning technique that limits the log loss by adding weak learning models.

Additionally, we have used deep learning models. Input, hidden, and output layers are the three layers that make up a standard deep learning model. Neurons in the input layer match the characteristics of the labeled data. Algorithms use unidentified components in the input distribution during the training system to extract features, group objections, and identify valuable data patterns. Optimization approach, Network architecture, and hyperparameter selection are crucial in deciding how well a neural network performs. The formula in Eq. (4) indicates how to calculate the activation function using the values of the hyperparameters.

$$a^i = g\left(x^i W_x + b_x\right) \tag{4}$$

In formula Eq. (4), a weightiness Wx is associated with the input atmosphere xi, and bx is the bias.

3.2 Multi classification algorithms

We proposed a multi-classification algorithm wherein we have used the following algorithms.

3.2.1 Multinomial logistic regression

Multinomial Logistic Regression is the multi-class version of logistic regression used for binary classification. This algorithm was practical when more than two classes were present. Moreover, it does not assume linearity, normality, and uniform error rates between independent and dependent variables. The number 0 stands for the weakest password, the number 1 for an average password, and the number 2 for the strongest password as shown in **Figures 2** and **3** below.

3.2.2 Decision trees

The independent variables create the decision tree, and each node has a characteristic condition. The node chooses which node to navigate next, depending on the circumstances. The output is projected once the leaf node has been reached. The tree is effective when the conditions are in the correct order. The tree structure is derived using a recursive greedy algorithm (**Figure 4**).

This enables the predictive models for accuracy, analysis, ease of use, and stability. This tool can also solve data-fitting problems such as classification and is effective for fitting non-linear relationships.

	password	strength
0	kzde5577	1
1	kino3434	1
2	visi7k1yr	1
3	megzy123	1
4	lamborghin1	1
5	AVYq1lDE4MgAZfNt	2
6	u6c8vhow	1
7	v1118714	1
8	universe2908	1
9	as326159	1
10	asv5o9yu	1
11	612035180tok	1
12	jytifok873	1
13	WUt9IZzE0OQ7PkNE	2
14	jerusalem393	1

Figure 2.
The first 15 elements of the dataset.

```
In [32]: from sklearn.linear_model import LogisticRegression
         clf=LogisticRegression(random_state=0,multi_class='multinomial',n_jobs=5)
         clf.fit(X_train,y_train)
         y_pred=clf.predict(X_test)
         y_pred
```

Figure 3.
Implementation of logistic regression.

```
: # Decision Tree model
  from sklearn.tree import DecisionTreeClassifier

  # instantiate the model
  tree = DecisionTreeClassifier(max_depth = 5)
  # fit the model
  tree.fit(X_train, y_train)

: DecisionTreeClassifier(max_depth=5)

: y_test_tree = tree.predict(X_test)
  y_train_tree = tree.predict(X_train)
```

Figure 4.
Implementation of decision tree.

```
In [38]: from xgboost import XGBClassifier

         # instantiate the model
         xgb = XGBClassifier(learning_rate=0.4,max_depth=7)
         #fit the model
         xgb.fit(X_train, y_train)

         [23:37:34] WARNING: C:/Users/Administrator/workspace/xgboost-win64_release_1
         0, the default evaluation metric used with the objective 'multi:softprob' wa:
         et eval_metric if you'd like to restore the old behavior.

Out[38]: XGBClassifier(base_score=0.5, booster='gbtree', colsample_bylevel=1,
                       colsample_bynode=1, colsample_bytree=1, gamma=0, gpu_id=-1,
                       importance_type='gain', interaction_constraints='',
                       learning_rate=0.4, max_delta_step=0, max_depth=7,
                       min_child_weight=1, missing=nan, monotone_constraints='()',
                       n_estimators=100, n_jobs=12, num_parallel_tree=1,
                       objective='multi:softprob', random_state=0, reg_alpha=0,
                       reg_lambda=1, scale_pos_weight=None, subsample=1,
                       tree_method='exact', validate_parameters=1, verbosity=None)

In [39]:
         #predicting the target value from the model for the samples
         y_test_xgb = xgb.predict(X_test)
         y_train_xgb = xgb.predict(X_train)
```

Figure 5.
Implementation of Xgboost.

```
In [27]: from sklearn.neural_network import MLPClassifier
         mlp=MLPClassifier((300,),activation='relu',verbose=1,
                           solver='adam',
                           batch_size=32,
                           learning_rate='constant',
                           learning_rate_init=0.001,
                           max_iter=20)
         mlp=mlp.fit(X_train,y_train)
```

Figure 6.
Implementation of MLP.

3.2.3 xgboost

Xgboost algorithm is in the form of an ensemble decision tree. It contains gradient boosting, which is helpful for regression and classification. Since the ensemble version of the decision tree is the boosted version of the original tree, Xgboost can provide better performance than decision trees (**Figure 5**).

3.2.4 Multilayer perceptron

It is a neural network used for prediction purposes. The perceptron is a single-neuron model pioneer of more extensive neural networks. The neurons are the smallest unit of a neural network, and the activation function defines their output. In our model, we have used 300 neurons, which rely upon the activation function to create our MLP model (**Figure 6**).

3.2.5 Keras

Keras is the TensorFlow library's artificial neural network interface [27]. Keras contains numerous features and is a good option for deep learning. In our Keras model, we have created two hidden layers with 300 neurons in each and a three-neuron output layer (**Figures 7** and **8**).

```
Ann1.add(tf.keras.layers.Dense(units=300,activation='relu'))
Ann1.add(tf.keras.layers.Dense(units=300,activation='relu'))
Ann1.add(tf.keras.layers.Dense(units=3,activation=tf.keras.activations.softm
ax))
Ann1.compile1(optimizer='adam',
        Loss1=tf.keras.losses.SparseCategoricalCrossentropy( ),
metrics =['accuracy'])
history=ann1.fit(X_train1_ann,np.array(y_train1),batch_size=37,
verbose=1,epochs=16)
```

Figure 7.
Implementation of Keras.

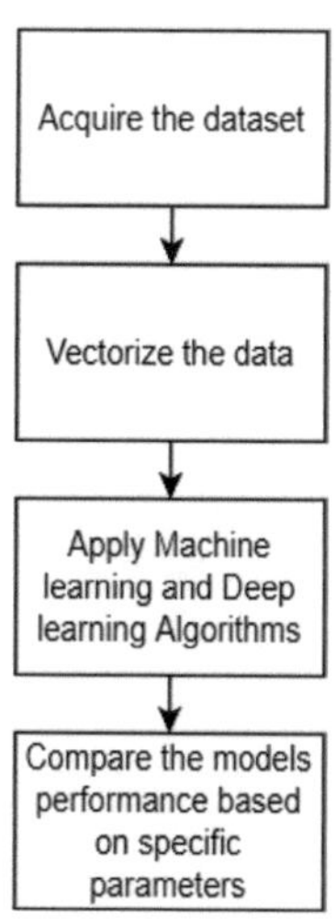

Figure 8.
Flowchart representing steps of the proposed multi-classification-based password strength prediction.

4. Result

The various models were implemented with Python and compared based on performance metrics. Out of all the algorithms, we found that the Keras model has the highest accuracy and outperformed every other model used in this work. We measured the performance using the classification report (which contains a precision, recall, and f-measure score), accuracy, and log loss.

4.1 Clustering report

This description comprehends the precision, recall, and f- f-measure scores for each of the passwords' three classes (weak, average, strong). The precision tells you how many of the correctly predicted situations ended up being positive. It was determined using this formula: The precision tells how many predicted situations were positive. This formula was used to calculate it.:

$$Precision = TP / (TP + FP) \tag{5}$$

The recall indicates how many of the actual positive cases of our model were able to predict the class correctly (**Figure 9**).

It was calculated using the below-given formula (6):

$$Recall = TP / (FN + TP) \tag{6}$$

4.2 F1-measure or F score

To create a single measure encompassing all properties, precision and recall were combined using the F-Measure. Below is the formula that was employed.

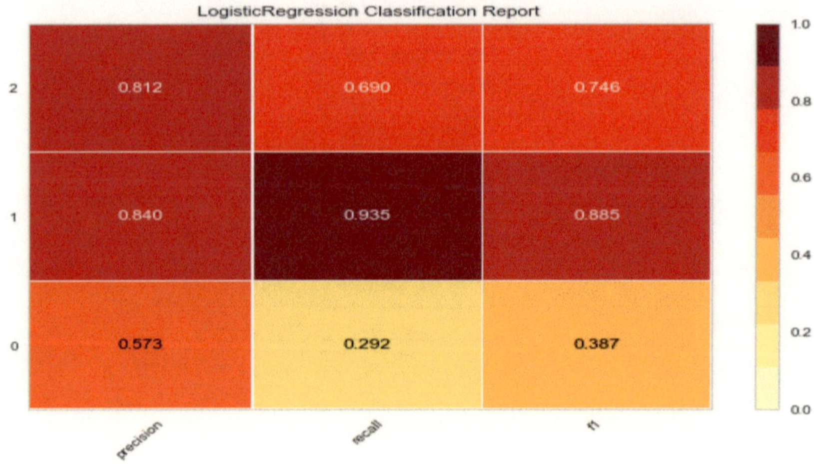

Figure 9.
Logistic regression classification report.

$$F - measure = (2 \times Precision \times Recall) / (Precision + Recall) \quad (7)$$

From **Figures 10** and **11**, we can infer that the precision, recall, and f-measure scores of Xgboost and MLP are very close for the three classes. The recall and f-measure scores of Xgboost are more significant than those of MLP, but the precision score for the weak passwords of the MLP classifier outperforms Xgboost. In **Figure 11**, only the recall score for weak passwords and the f1 score for weak passwords are higher compared to **Figure 12**. In **Figure 10**, the f1 scores are lower compared to **Table 1**, along with the recall scores for weak and strong passwords.

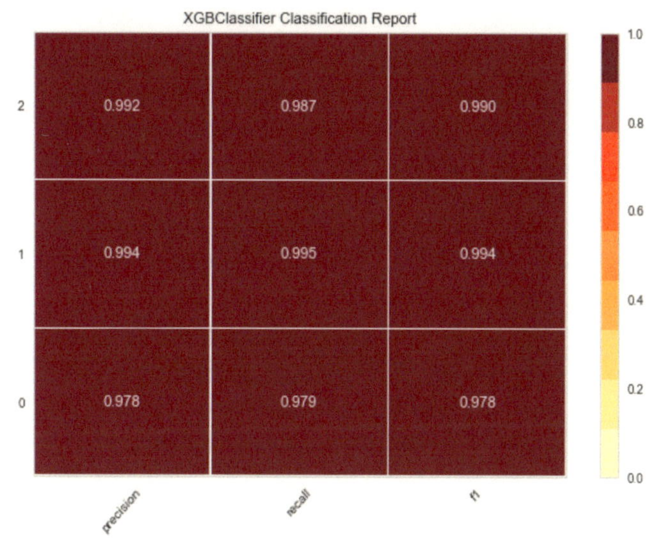

Figure 10.
Xgboost classification report.

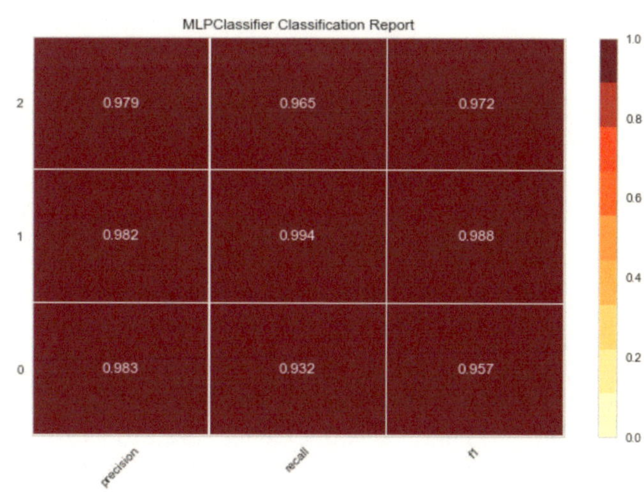

Figure 11.
MLP classification report.

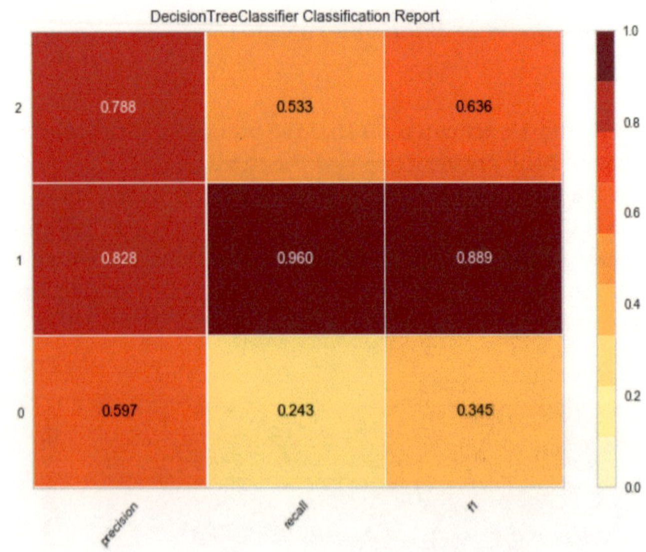

Figure 12.
Decision tree classification report.

Classes	Classification report		
	Precision	Recall	F1
0(weak)	0.974	0.985	0.980
1(average)	0.992	0.993	0.993
2(strong)	0.991	0.969	0.980

Table 1.
Keras classification report.

Hence, Xgboost has scored the highest in most classes, followed by Keras and MLP, who have performed similarly. Decision trees have performed better than logistic regression, which is the lowest performer.

4.3 Accuracy score

The accuracy score is applied to test data to calculate the True Positive percentage. Using this formula, the accuracy of the three models was calculated (**Figure 13**).

$$\text{Accuracy} = (\text{TP} + \text{TN}) / (\text{TP} + \text{FP} + \text{TN} + \text{FN}) \tag{8}$$

From **Table 2** below, we can conclude that Xgboost outperforms every other model used, followed by Keras, MLP, Logistic Regression, and Decision tree, which has performed the worst. The neural network models' performance is better than the machine learning models' as they make predictions without learning, unlike machine learning algorithms.

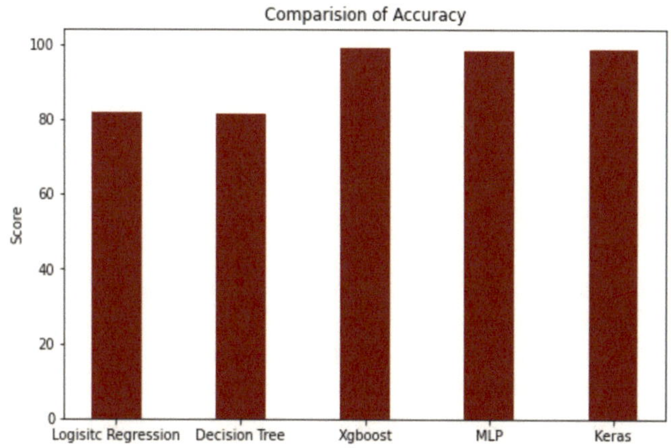

Figure 13.
Accuracy comparison graph.

Sl. No	Algorithms	Score
1	Logistic regression	81.8
2	Decision tree	81.4
3	xgboost	99.2
4	MLP	98.4
5	Keras	98.9

Table 2.
Accuracy scores.

4.4 Log loss

Log loss score is a handy metric to compare the performance of a model with other models based on classification. Log loss makes it easier to interpret raw log-loss values. It is the opposing average of corrected probabilities. It is given by the formula Eq. (9).

$$\log loss = -1/N\sum_{i=1}^{N}.\left(\log\left(Pi\right)\right) \quad (9)$$

Sl. No	Algorithms	Score
1	Logistic regression	0.411515
2	Decision tree	0.539443
3	xgboost	0.038219
4	MLP	0.058158
5	Keras	0.039329

Table 3.
Loss function scores.

Low Log loss values convey that the model has provided better predictions, but a higher value shows that the model provides terrible predictions.

From **Table 3** above, we can infer that Xgboost has shown the most minor loss while Decision Tree has the highest, making it the least performing among the five models.

5. Conclusions

Keras, MLP, and logistic regression are the best models after Xgboost. Xgboost performed better than the two neural networks employed in the proposed method. Xgboost's gradient boosting capability enabled it to provide a higher score. When faced with diverse data, Xgboost performs better than neural networks. Our dataset has various features that make it ideal for Xgboost to learn from, making it a superior option to neural networks. We must amend these regulations since we also determine that steganography passwords formed using the policy of using more than eight characters, including one lowercase, one uppercase, and one number, may be weak. Here, we present a deep learning and machine learning algorithm-based technique for determining a steganography password's strengths, weaknesses, and average. Steganography passwords and their strengths make up the dataset that we have utilized. We have employed the TF-IDF approach to convert the dataset into vectors for improved machine learning and deep learning algorithm performance. Each model's output was calculated using the proposed approach, and the results were compared. The machine learning algorithm Xgboost has been proven to exhibit the highest accuracy and outperform other machine learning and deep learning algorithms in this work. To safeguard your private data on the internet in this day and age, you should make a unique password for each site. A secure password must include the following essential elements: uniqueness, length, capital, lowercase, and numeric characters. Even though it could appear difficult. Through the use of proposed method, the user can more easily determine whether their password poses a security concern by simulating its strength evaluation value. Large datasets are scraped and gathered by our suggested system, which is then utilized to both provide a user-friendly mechanism to assist users in creating strong passwords and test the strength of user passwords based on known password strength criteria. The effectiveness of the suggested meter in encouraging users to establish more secure passwords is how we assess our system.

Author details

V. Balaji* and P. Selvaraj
Department of Computing Technologies, Faculty of Engineering and Technology, College of Engineering and Technology, SRM Institute of Science and Technology, Kattankulathur, Chennai, TN, India

*Address all correspondence to: bv0089@srmist.edu.in

References

[1] Torvi SD, ShivaKumar KB, Das R. An unique data security using text steganography. In: 2016 3rd International Conference on Computing for Sustainable Global Development (INDIACom); New Delhi, India. IEEE Xplore; 2016. pp. 3834-3838. Article Number 7724977

[2] Johri P, Mishra A, Das S, Kumar A. Survey on steganography methods (text, image, audio, video, protocol and network steganography). In: 2016 3rd International Conference on Computing for Sustainable Global Development (INDIACom); New Delhi, India. IEEE Xplore; 2016. pp. 2906-2909. Article Number 7724795

[3] Rabiner L, Juang B. An introduction to hidden Markov models. IEEE ASSP Magazine. 1986;**3**(1):4-16

[4] Castelluccia C, Dürmuth M, Perito D. Adaptive password-strength meters from markov models. In: NDSS. The Internet Society; 2012

[5] Guo Y, Zhang Z. LPSE: Lightweight password-strength estimation for password meters. Computers & Security. 2018;**73**:507-518

[6] Seitz T, Hussmann H. PASDJO: Quantifying Password Strength Perceptions with an Online Game. 2017. pp. 117-125. DOI: 10.1145/3152771.3152784

[7] Wheeler DL. zxcvbn: Low-budget password strength estimation. In: Holz T, Savage S, editors. USENIX Security Symposium. USENIX Association; 2016. pp. 157-173

[8] Doucek P et al. Adaptation of password strength estimators to a non-English environment—The Czech experience. Computers & Security. 2020;**95**:101757

[9] Vijaya MS, Jamuna KS, Karpagavalli S. Password strength prediction using supervised machine learning techniques. In: Advances in Computing, Control, and Telecommunication Technologies, International Conference on. 2009. pp. 401-405. DOI: 10.1109/ACT.2009.105

[10] Hitaj B et al. Passgan: A deep learning approach for password guessing. In: International Conference on Applied Cryptography and Network Security. Cham: Springer; 2019

[11] Bauer L, Melicher W, Ur B, Segreti S, Komanduri S, Christin N, et al. Fast, lean, and accurate: Modeling password guessability using neural networks. In: Christin N, Cranor L, editors. USENIX Security Symposium. 2016. pp. 175-191

[12] Xu M, Han W. An explainable password strength meter addon via textual pattern recognition. Security and Communication Networks. 2019;**2019**:5184643, 1-10

[13] Abdrabou Y, Abdelrahman Y, Khamis M, Alt F. Think Harder! Investigating the Effect of Password Strength on Cognitive Load during Password Creation. 2021. pp. 1-7. DOI: 10.1145/3411763.3451636

[14] Egelman S, Sotirakopoulos A, Muslukhov I, Beznosov K, Herley C. Does my password go up to eleven?: The impact of password meters on password selection. In: Conference on Human Factors in Computing Systems - Proceedings. 2013. pp. 2379-2388. DOI: 10.1145/2470654.2481329

[15] Pereira D, Ferreira JF, Mendes A. Evaluating the accuracy of password strength meters using off-the-shelf guessing attacks. In: 2020 IEEE International Symposium on Software Reliability Engineering Workshops (ISSREW), Coimbra, Portugal. 2020. pp. 237-242. DOI: 10.1109/ISSREW51248.2020.00079

[16] Pasquini D, Ateniese G, Bernaschi M. Interpretable probabilistic password strength meters via deep learning. In: European Symposium on Research in Computer Security. Cham: Springer; 2020

[17] Melicher W et al. Fast, lean, and accurate: Modeling password guessability using neural networks. In: 25th {USENIX} Security Symposium ({USENIX} Security 16). 2016. pp. 175-191

[18] Kariryaa A, Schöning J. MoiPrivacy: Design and Evaluation of a Personal Password Meter. 2020. DOI: 10.1145/3428361.3428397

[19] Hanamsagar A, Woo S, Kanich C, Mirkovic J. Leveraging Semantic Transformation to Investigate Password Habits and Their Causes. 2018. pp. 1-12. DOI: 10.1145/3173574.3174144

[20] Bojinov H et al. Kamouflage: Loss-resistant password management. In: European Symposium on Research in Computer Security. Berlin, Heidelberg: Springer; 2010

[21] Pal B, Daniel T, Chatterjee R, Ristenpart T. Beyond Credential Stuffing: Password Similarity Models Using Neural Networks. 2019. pp. 417-434. DOI: 10.1109/SP.2019.00056

[22] Einziger G, Goldstein M, Sa'ar Y, Segall I. Verifying robustness of gradient boosted models. In: Proceedings of the AAAI Conference on Artificial Intelligence. Vol. 33, No. 1. 2019. pp. 2446-2453. DOI: 10.1609/aaai.v33i01.33012446

[23] He Y, Alem EE, Wang W. Hybritus: A password strength checker by ensemble learning from the query feedbacks of websites. Frontiers of Computer Science. 2020;**14**(3):1-14

[24] Bai W, Blocki J, Harsha B. Password strength signaling: A counter-intuitive defense against password cracking. In: International Conference on Decision and Game Theory for Security. Cham: Springer; 2021

[25] Aratani A, Kanai A. Authentication method against shoulder-surfing attacks using secondary channel. In: 2015 IEEE International Conference on Consumer Electronics, ICCE 2015. 2015. pp. 430-431. DOI: 10.1109/ICCE.2015.7066474

[26] Bansal B. Password-Strength-Classifier-Dataset. Available from: https://www.kaggle.com/bhavikbb/password-strength-classifier-dataset

[27] Abadi M, Agarwal A, Barham P, Brevdo E. TensorFlow: Large-Scale Machine Learning on Heterogeneous Systems. 2015. Available from: https://www.tensorflow.org/

Chapter 6

Encryption Scheme for the Security of Digital Images Based on Josephus Traversal and Chaos Theory

Manzoor Lone

Abstract

A synergistic approach based on the Josephus traversal and chaos theory is suggested for the security of digital images. To encrypt the digital images, a combination of the Josephus Traversal principle and the 2-dimensional Hénon map is employed for the secure transmission of digital data. The two distinct key matrices are used in the Josephus principle to cause bit-level shuffling throughout the image. These two distinct key matrices are effectively formed by the chaotic streams generated by the two-dimensional Hénon map. The system becomes more unpredictable because the Josephus traversal employs a different key set for every individual pixel to scramble it at the bit level. Moreover, the image is shuffled and diffused at the pixel level using the same streams produced by chaotic structure. The test images are used to determine the strength of the suggested system. The numerical results and comparative findings of the various quality parameters such as key space, information entropy, correlation coefficient, histogram analysis, differential attack indicators (NPCR and UACI) verify the strength of the encryption system. The acceptable key space, numerical values of entropy approaches to ideal value, correlation coefficient values close to 0, and satisfactory results of theoretical value tests verify the robustness of the employed scheme to resist various types of cryptanalytical attacks.

Keywords: security, Josephus traversal, encryption, 2D Hénon map, confusion, diffusion

1. Introduction

Encryption process transforms the information (plain-text) into a non-readable format (cipher-text) using some well-defined encryption method. The unauthorized persons without the prior knowledge of secret keys used in the encryption process are unable to recover the original information [1]. The digital data communicated over the internet always experience the risk of security. Thus, for a smooth and effective delivery system, sensitive and private data always needs to be masked and protected before transmission over the internet [2]. Multimedia content, such as digital images, plays an important role in the e-healthcare system, e-governance, e-commerce, e-education, e-banking, and in other fields of human life. Therefore, to ensure the safe communication of data, a secure transmission method needs to be designed and developed. The security paradigms, such as watermarking, cryptography, steganography, and so forth, are applied to impart security to the data communicated over insecure internet channels. A large number of encryption algorithms have been fabricated by researchers using techniques such as wavelet transform, chaos theory, DNA encoding, cellular automata, and others. Among them, the encryption methods based on chaos theory for the fabrication of data security algorithms is a fundamental alluring option used by researchers. In recent years, various encryption schemes for digital images based on chaotic maps have been suggested [3–14]. These schemes either use low-dimensional and high-dimensional chaotic maps, or a mixture of them, or enhance the existing chaotic structures, or combine them with other techniques to encrypt the digital images. In [10], the suggested encryption scheme uses a single chaotic map, the Arnold map, to generate the final cipher image. In the encryption scheme, the scrambling and diffusion of pixels are achieved by using the Arnold map. In [15], the encryption method first uses the Chebyshev map to diffuse and shuffle pixels, and then, it applies the modified Logistic map to mask and confuse the pixels simultaneously. This scheme has fine pseudorandomness and is resistant to different types of attacks. In [16], the encryption scheme combines chaos theory and elliptic curve ElGamal (EC-ElGamal) to secure digital image communication. The scheme not only enhances the security of the encryption system but also addresses key management problem. In [17], a new 2D cosine map is proposed that has fine ergodicity, a more perplexing nature, more randomness, and a large chaotic range compared to the existing 2D chaotic map. In [11], the proposed encryption method uses the 1D logistic map and Josephus traversal principle to produce a reliable cipher image. The scheme is highly sensitive to initial value conditions that boost the security of the system.

In [18], the encryption method uses chaotic structures and DNA encoding with a one-time pad to confuse and diffuse the digital images. First, the image is shuffled, and the shuffled image is divided into four sub-images of equal sizes, and DNA rules encode these sub-images and diffuse them, respectively. The diffusion process is obtained by DNA XOR operations, and at last, these sub-images are joined to form the cipher image. The algorithm provides resistance to typical attacks and has good security. In [19], the suggested scheme uses variable step Josephus traversal and a Y-index Space Filling Curve (SFC) to provide an effective and enhanced image encryption security algorithm. The numerical findings and the comparison results of the proposed algorithm depict that this scheme has good security than others. In [2], the encryption scheme uses a combined approach of chaotic maps and the Affine Hill Cipher method to generate a secure cipher. In the first two stages of encryption, the input image is shuffled and diffused by the application of the 2-dimensional Hénon map and the 3-dimensional logistic map, respectively. Finally, the application of the AHC technique produces a strong cipher image. In [20], authors proposed an encryption scheme based on chaotic systems, hash function, and Josephus traversal concept. The encryption method applies chaotic system initialization, pixel shuffling, and pixel diffusion to form a cipher image. The system has effective security and efficiently combats against various attacks.

Inspired by the above literature study, the suggested scheme couples chaotic structure 2D Hénon map with Josephus traversal principle to form an encryption framework. The suggested scheme first brings bit-shuffling in all the pixels of the plain image with help of the Josephus traversal. After it, the confusion and diffusion in the pixels of the image is carried by using the two chaotic streams R_s^x and R_s^y, respectively, generated by the 2D Hénon map. Further, the two chaotic sequences generated by the 2D Hénon map are used in a novel way to generate the key matrices for Josephus traversal. The Josephus traversal is operated on each individual pixel at the bit level. It uses a distinct key set for every pixel to trigger the bit-level scrambling in the image data. The key set used for the shuffling of bits in each individual pixel by the Josephus traversal is derived from the two chaotic sequences generated by the 2D Hénon map. The variable key set notion used in the Josephus traversal improves the overall randomness and unpredictability, thus enhancing the performance and security of the proposed system. The initial key parameter of the chaotic system is related to the plain image, which greatly increases the security of the system. The small change in such dependencies brings an avalanche in the output of a cryptosystem. Further, the favorable key space, satisfactory results of correlation coefficient, entropy results, differential attack indicator (NPCR and UACI) results, and uniform histograms of cipher images determine the strength of the proposed image encryption system.

2. Preliminaries

2.1 Two-dimensional Hénon map

Michel Hénon in 1976 introduced the concept of the 2-dimensional Hénon map in [21]. It is a model of a nonlinear discrete-time dynamical system showing chaos defined on a 2D plane. The 2D Hénon map is employed in various image security approaches [22–24]. Following is the mathematical relation of the map:

$$\begin{cases} R^x_{s+1} = 1 - \rho_1 \times R^x_s + R^y_s, \\ R^y_{s+1} = \rho_2 \times R^x_s, \end{cases} \tag{1}$$

where represent the initial conditions, and parameters ρ_1 and ρ_2 are known as bifurcation parameters. For $\rho_1 \in [0,1.4]$, $\rho_2 = 0.3$, the bifurcation characteristic nature of the Hénon map can be observed and is generally investigated at $\rho_1 = 1.4$ and $\rho_2 = 0.3$ as shown in **Figures 1** and **2**. The extent of thickness and stretching is governed by the bifurcation parameters (ρ_1, ρ_2) also named as chaotic attractors.

2.2 Josephus problem

The Josephus traversal is a famous problem in Computer Science and Mathematics [13, 25–28]. The problem is named after a Jewish historian Flavius Josephus. It represents a theoretical problem that is similar to a counting-out player game. In this game, there are n players in a circular pattern. Traverse the circle in a predetermined direction and start at a pre-specified first x^{th} person, eliminating the first person. After the first person is eliminated, then a predefined step count is used to skip a certain number of persons in the already predefined direction and eliminate the second person. The procedure continues, starting with the next person, following the same direction and using the same step count to skip persons till the last person is left. In the end, the persons eliminated from the circle, starting at a specified position, in a predetermined order and with a predetermined step count form a sequence known as the Josephus traversal sequence. Hence, the Josephus traversal contains three parameters n, x, and c, where n is the total number of players in the game, x is starting person, and c is the step count to skip the certain number of persons in a pre-specified direction. Thus, the Josephus traversal is represented by function $\mathcal{R}_{\odot} = J(n, x, c)$, where $\mathcal{R}_{\odot}$ represents the Josephus traversal sequence. For example, the solution to $\mathcal{R}_{\odot} = J(7,1,2)$, where $n = 7$ with 1, 2, 3, 4, 5, 6, 7 makes a circle, $x = 1$ and $c = 4$, we obtain the Josephus traversal sequence $\mathcal{R}_{\odot} = 4, 1, 6, 5, 7, 3, 2$.

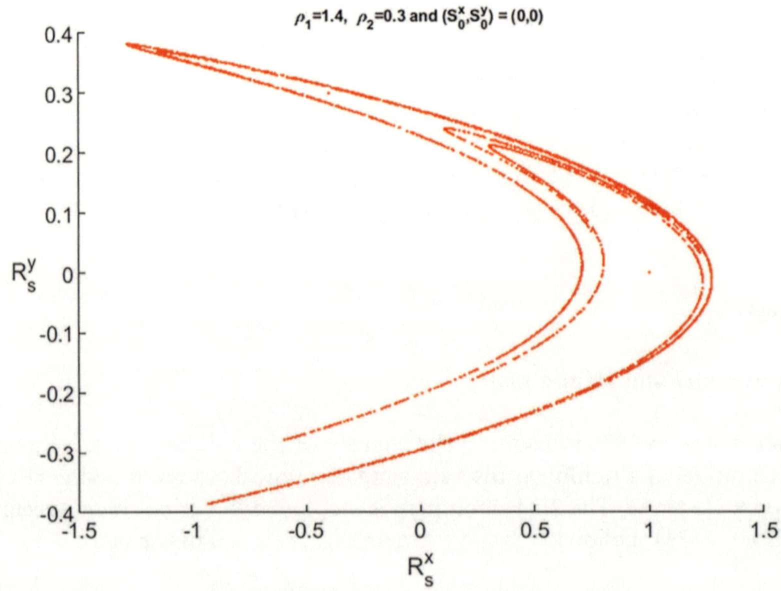

Figure 1.
2D Hénon attractor.

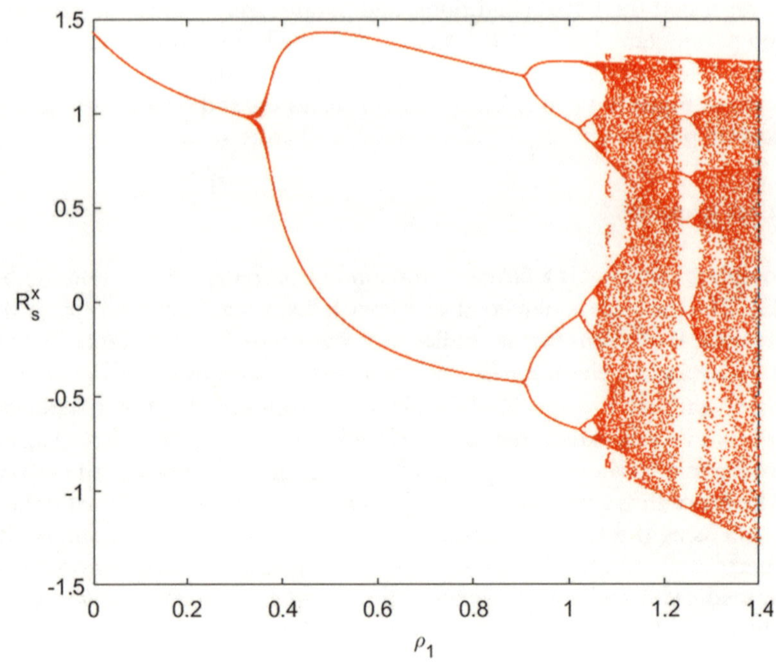

Figure 2.
2D Hénon map's bifurcation plot.

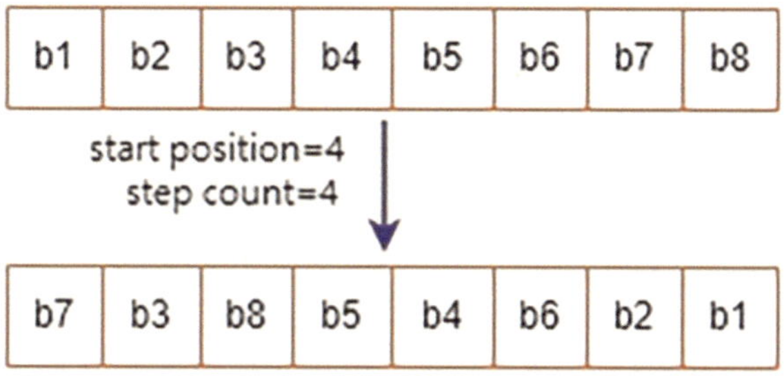

Figure 3.
Bit shuffling using Josephus traversal, when starting position = 4 and step count = 4.

To enhance the randomness and unpredictability in the Josephus traversal sequence, the literature [11–13, 20, 29, 30] motivated to exploit a similar type of pattern to raise the degree of randomness in the Josephus traversal. The distinct starting positions and the distinct step counts for the Josephus traversal are determined from R_s^x and R_s^y chaotic sequences, respectively, generated by the two-dimensional Hénon map. The two chaotic sequences R_s^x and R_s^y are scaled in the range of [1–8] and transformed into two matrices $[M_s]$ and $[M_c]$ of the same dimensions as the original image. $[M_s]$ work as the starting position key matrix, and $[M_c]$ act as the step count key matrix. In the proposed scheme, the element from $[M_s]$ and $[M_c]$ frame the key set for Josephus traversal to operate the bit shuffling in one pixel of the plain image. Likewise, to bring the bit shuffling in all pixels, key sets are derived for Josephus traversal from $[M_s]$ and $[M_c]$. Thus, distinct key sets for all individual pixels of the image are framed and applied to cause bit shuffling in each pixel, as demonstrated in **Figure 3**, respectively. This feature enhances the security of the proposed scheme system.

3. Initialization and encryption process

The assignment process of initial conditions of the 2D Hénon map and the proposed encryption algorithm are elaborated in this section.

3.1 Initialization of chaotic structure

The initial value conditions of the 2-dimensional Hénon map are made dependent on the plain image data. In such relations, a small change produces an avalanche in the cipher, hence ensuring protection against cryptanalytical attacks. The key generation pattern discussed in [31] inspired author to initialize the initial values of the 2-dimensional Hénon map shown as follows:

$k = (1/(row * col * 255)) * (\sum img);$

if $(k \geq 1)$

$R_0^x = \mathbf{mod}(k, 1);$

else.

$R_0^x = k;$

end if

$R_0^y = (R_0^x/2);$

3.2 Encryption process

The proposed algorithm are elaborated in this section. The values of R_0^x, R_0^y, ρ_1, and ρ_2 represent the secret key parameters in the suggested system. The steps followed in the suggested encryption system are listed below:

Algorithm-I

Step 1: Transform the input image $[img_o]$ into the binary form image, say $[img^{Bin}]$.
Step 2: Apply Hénon map using Eq. (1) and generate two chaotic sequence R_s^x and R_s^y.
Step 3: Scale both the sequences R_s^x and R_s^y in the range of [1–8] and transform them into matrices, say $[M_s]$ and $[M_c]$, respectively.
Step 4: $[M_s]$ and $[M_c]$ are employed as distinct key set matrices for the Josephus traversal technique.
Step 5: Apply the Josephus traversal process as discussed in subsection 2.2 on the binary image produced in step 2.

$$[img^{BinScrmb}] \underset{\text{Traversal}}{\overset{\text{Josephus}}{\longleftarrow}} [img^{Bin}]$$

Step 6: Transform $[img^{BinScrmb}]$ into decimal form, say $[img']$.
Step 7: In this step, apply **Sort** index function to $[R_s^x]$ sequences generated in step 3 and shuffle all the pixels of the image as shown in the following pseudo-code: $[val \quad inx]{:=}sort(R_s^x)$; $[img''] = [img'](inx)$; Transform $[img'']$ into a matrix.
Step 8: Select the $[R_s^y]$ sequences generated in step 3 and scale it in the range of [0–255] and transform the scaled output into a matrix of $row * col$ dimension, say $[R^y]_{row*col}$.
Step 9: Perform XOR operation between $[img'']$ and $[R^y]$. This causes diffusion in the final image, and at the end, an encrypted image img^C is acquired.

Thus, at the end of the procedure, we obtain a cipher image img^C. The reconstruction of the original in the decryption process is obtained by following the inverse of all the steps followed in the encryption process.

---

4. Result analysis

The results of the proposed system for various indicators are calculated using grayscale images shown in **Figure 4**. The size of the images is 256 × 256. MATLAB tool with a machine having Windows 10 and IntelR, CoreTM i7 CPU 2.40GHz and 16GB is used for the simulation purpose.

4.1 Key space

The key space of an encryption algorithm is a vital security parameter. It should be large enough to counter brute force attacks. According to the literature study [32], key space $\geq 2^{128}$ is safe to resist exhaustive attacks. With a precision of 2^{-15}, the total key space of the proposed algorithm is 2^{199}, which is reliable to resist brute force attacks effectively.

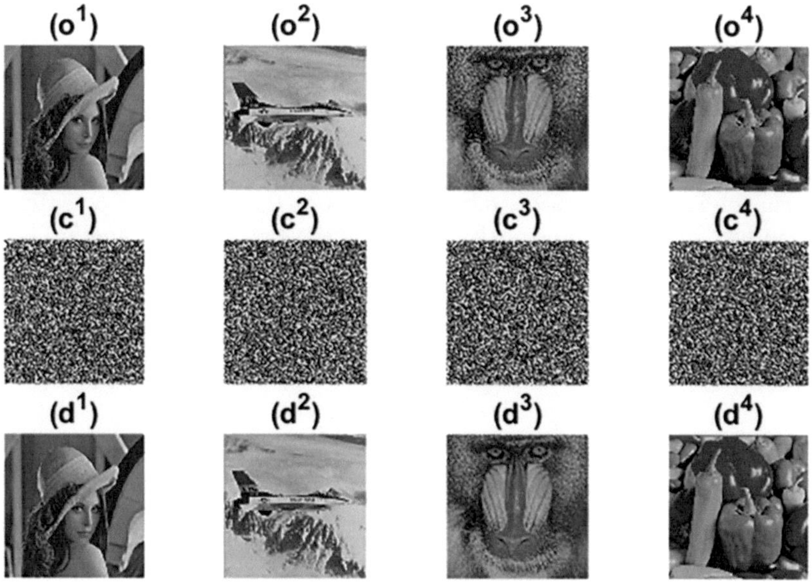

Figure 4.
o^1-o^4 = plain images, c^1-c^4 = cipher images, d^1-d^4 = decrypted images.

4.2 Information entropy

The information entropy evaluation reflects the unpredictability and randomness of data. The values of entropy closer to the theoretical value of 8 for 2^8 gray-level image determine strong randomness in cipher data [33]. Eq. (2) represents the mathematical formula of information entropy:

$$\mathcal{IE}_{(\mathcal{S})} = -\sum_{v=0}^{255} p(\mathcal{S}_v)\, log\,_2 p(\mathcal{S}_v), \tag{2}$$

where, $\mathcal{S}_v$ = source symbol, and $p(\mathcal{S}_v)$ = probability of source symbol. The numerical results of $\mathcal{IE}_{(\mathcal{S})}$ listed in **Table 1** are close to the theoretical value 8, ensuring high randomness in the cipher data generated by the proposed encryption scheme.

Image	Entropy
Lena	7.9974
Jet	7.9969
Mandrill	7.9974
Pepper	7.9972

Table 1.
Information entropy results.

4.3 Differential attack

In this analysis, a little change is caused in the plain image, and then, the two images are encrypted by some predefined method. Through this investigation, the attacker attempts to know the link between plain image and cipher image. The two indicators, namely, NPCR (number of pixels change rate) and UACI (unified average changed intensity), are two basic parameters that decide the potential of an encryption system to withstand against differential attacks. Eq. (3) and Eq. (4) represent the two indicators, respectively [25].

$$NPCR = \frac{1}{row * col} \sum_{s_1, s_2} D_{(s_1, s_2)} * 100\% \tag{3}$$

$$D_{(s_1,s_2)} = \begin{cases} 1 & \text{if } img'_{(s_1,s_2)} \neq img''_{(s_1,s_2)} \\ 0 & \text{otherwise} \end{cases}$$

$$UACI = \frac{1}{(row * col)} * X * 100\%, \tag{4}$$

$$\text{where,} \quad X = \sum_{s_1, s_2} \frac{|img'_{(s_1,s_2)} - img''_{(s_1,s_2)}|}{255}$$

Table 2 depicts the results of NPCR and UACI parameters and are in close proximity to their reference values. Hence, justify that the suggested scheme can resist differential attacks satisfactorily.

		$\mathcal{N}^*_{0.05}$	$\mathcal{N}^*_{0.01}$	$\mathcal{N}^*_{0.001}$ [34]
Image	NPCR	99.5693	99.5527	99.5341
Lena	99.6368	✓	✓	✓
Jet	99.6262	✓	✓	✓
Mandrill	99.6002	✓	✓	✓
Pepper	99.5804	✓	✓	✓
Avg.=	99.6110	✓	✓	✓
		$V^{*-}_{0.05}$	$V^{*-}_{0.01}$	$V^{*-}_{0.001}$ [20]
		$V^{*+}_{0.05}$	$V^{*+}_{0.01}$	$V^{*+}_{0.001}$
		33.2824	33.2255	33.1594
Image	UACI	33.6447	33.7016	33.7677
Lena	33.5372	✓	✓	✓
Jet	33.3475	✓	✓	✓
Mandrill	33.6070	✓	✓	✓
Pepper	33.4553	✓	✓	✓
Avg.=	33.4868	✓	✓	✓

Table 2.
Results of NPCR and UACI indicators.

4.4 Correlation analysis

In an encrypted image, the correlation among the adjoining pixels in horizontal, vertical, and diagonal directions should be 0 or approaching to 0. If the correlation is mitigated, it is hard for an attacker to crack the cipher using statistical analysis. The correlation coefficient $\psi_{s^x s^y}$ [22] is used to conduct this analysis, represented by Eq. (5).

$$\begin{cases} \psi_{s^x s^y} &= \mathbb{C}_{(s^x, s^y)} / \left(\sqrt{D(s^x)}^* \sqrt{D(s^y)}\right), \\ \mathbb{C}_{(s^x, s^y)} &= (1/N) * \sum_{i=1}^{N} {}^* F \\ F &= \left(s_i^x - E(s^x)\right) * \left(s_i^y - E(s^y)\right) \\ D(s^x) &= (1/N) * \sum_{i=1}^{N} \left(s_i^x - E(s^x)\right)^2, \\ E(s^x) &= (1/N) * \sum_{i=1}^{N} \left(s_i^x\right) \end{cases} \tag{5}$$

The correlation coefficient results of the encrypted image in **Table 3** are close to 0 along the horizontal (H), vertical (V), and diagonal (D) axis. **Figure 5** shows the correlation plots of plain and cipher images. It is obvious from **Figure 5** that the data is highly correlated in the plain image, and in contrast to it, the data in cipher image is strongly uncorrelated. Thus, it reveals that the proposed system is able to counter statistical attacks effectively.

Corr.	Lena	Jet	Mandrill	Pepper
VC	−0.0033	−0.0004	0.0002	0.0037
HC	−0.0054	−0.0064	0.0037	−0.0022
DC	0.0004	−0.0005	0.0045	−0.0002

Table 3.
Correlation coefficient results.

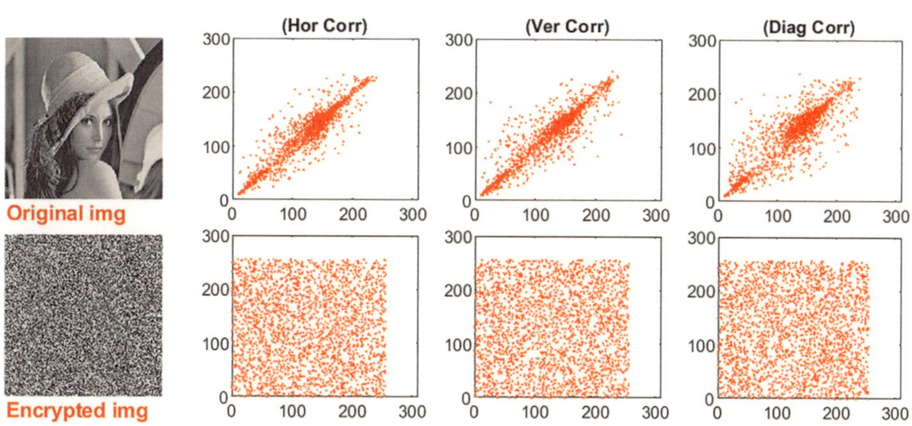

Figure 5.
Correlation plots.

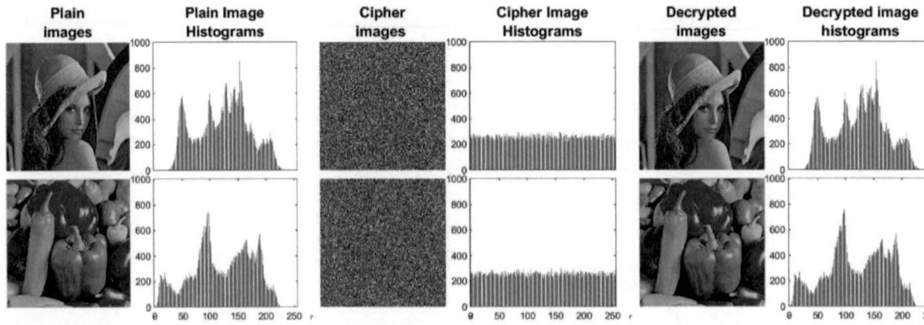

Figure 6.
Histogram plots.

4.5 Histogram analysis

The histogram distribution reveals important statistical information about an image. This information needs to be concealed in a cipher histogram, which is possible only if the encrypted image yields a flat histogram. If an encryption algorithm performs only pixel shuffling, the histogram of the image remains unaffected. Thus, the objective of the application of the bit-scrambling process and diffusion process in the proposed algorithm is to yield a uniform cipher histogram to counter the statistic attacks. Histogram plots of cipher and plain images are shown in **Figure 6**. It can be observed that histograms of cipher images are evenly distributed compared to the original images. Thus, the proposed algorithm masks the statistical information and results in an effective encryption system, which indicates that encrypted images yield uniform histograms. This ensures that the proposed security method can strongly counter the histogram based attacks.

5. Comparison results

The comparison results of the proposed scheme for entropy, NPCR, UACI, and correlation coefficient parameters are listed in **Table 4**. The comparative assessment shows that the outcomes of the suggested scheme are good, acceptable, and

Image	Algorithm	Entropy	NPCR	UACI	H_{Corr}	V_{Corr}	D_{Corr}
Lena	Proposed	7.9974	99.6368	33.5372	−0.0054	−0.0033	0.0004
	Ref. [35]	7.9972	99.6246	33.4226	0.0069	0.0479	0.0075
	Ref. [36]	7.9972	99.6124	33.4468	−0.0019	−0.00023	−0.00013
	Ref. [19]	7.9971	99.6337	33.6050	0.0071	−0.0052	0.0013
	Ref. [8]	7.9972	99.6262	33.4578	−0.0003	0.0016	0.0029
	Ref. [20]	7.9973	99.6117	33.4570	−0.0013	−0.0008	−0.0017
	Ref. [12]	7.9971	99.5989	33.4561	−0.0029	−0.0017	0.0004
	Ref. [37]	7.9975	99.6114	33.4636	−0.0223	−0.0084	−0.0086

Table 4.
Comparison results.

DOI: http://dx.doi.org/10.5772/intechopen.1005121

concurrent with the results of the existing encryption schemes. Thus, the comparative analysis also favors the robustness, stalwartness, and effectiveness of the suggested encryption scheme.

6. Conclusion

The work in this article exploits chaotic system and the principle of the Josephus traversal to encrypt digital images. The suggested scheme makes efficient and effective use of the chaotic streams generated by the 2D Hénon map to shuffle and diffuse the image at the pixel level. Simultaneously, at the bit level, the same chaotic streams of the 2D Hénon map are employed to form the distinct keys in the Josephus traversal to shuffle the bits of the pixels in the whole image. The results of the key space, entropy, and correlation coefficient are favorable. The theoretical value test of differential attack indicators (NPCR and UACI) depicted in **Table 2** is satisfactorily. Thus, the simulation analysis verifies that the security level of the suggested method is good and thus can be used in image encryption.

Author details

Manzoor Lone
Department of CSE, University of Kashmir (North Campus), India

*Address all correspondence to: mahmadlone@gmail.com

References

[1] Stinson DR. Cryptography: Theory and Practice. Boca Raton: CRC Press, Taylor & Francis Group; 2005

[2] Lone MA, Qureshi S. Encryption scheme for rgb images using chaos and affine hill cipher technique. Nonlinear Dynamics. 2022;**11**:1-21

[3] Belazi A, Talha M, Kharbech S, Xiang W. Novel medical image encryption scheme based on chaos and DNA encoding. IEEE Access. 2019;**7**: 36667-36681

[4] Farah M, Farah A, Farah T. An image encryption scheme based on a new hybrid chaotic map and optimized substitution box. Nonlinear Dynamics. 2020;**99**(4):3041-3064

[5] Li C, Luo G, Qin K, Li C. An image encryption scheme based on chaotic tent map. Nonlinear Dynamics. 2017;**87**(1): 127-133

[6] Lone MA, Qureshi S. Rgb image encryption based on symmetric keys using Arnold transform, 3d chaotic map and affine hill cipher. Optik. 2022;**260**: 168880

[7] Luo Y, Yu J, Lai W, Liu L. A novel chaotic image encryption algorithm based on improved baker map and logistic map. Multimedia Tools and Applications. 2019;**78**(15):22023-22043

[8] Niu Y, Zhang X. A novel plaintext-related image encryption scheme based on chaotic system and pixel permutation. IEEE Access. 2020;**8**:22082-22093

[9] Wu J, Cao X, Liu X, Ma L, Xiong J. Image encryption using the random frdct and the chaos-based game of life. Journal of Modern Optics. 2019;**66**(7): 764-775

[10] Wu J, Liu Z, Wang J, Hu L, Liu S. A compact image encryption system based on Arnold transformation. Multimedia Tools and Applications. 2021;**80**(2): 2647-2661

[11] Yang G, Jin H, Bai N. Image encryption using the chaotic Josephus matrix. Mathematical Problems in Engineering. 2014;**2014**:632060

[12] Wang X, Zhu X, Zhang Y. An image encryption algorithm based on Josephus traversing and mixed chaotic map. IEEE Access. 2018;**6**:23733-23746

[13] Yi G, Li-ping S, Lu Y. Bit-level image encryption algorithm based on Josephus and Henon chaotic map. Application Research of Computers/Jisuanji Yingyong Yanjiu. 2015;**32**(4):1-7

[14] Zhou Y, Hua Z, Pun C-M, Chen CP. Cascade chaotic system with applications. IEEE Transactions on Cybernetics. 2014;**45**(9):2001-2012

[15] Diab H. An efficient chaotic image cryptosystem based on simultaneous permutation and diffusion operations. IEEE Access. 2018;**6**:42227-42244

[16] Luo Y, Ouyang X, Liu J, Cao L. An image encryption method based on elliptic curve elgamal encryption and chaotic systems. IEEE Access. 2019;**7**: 38507-38522

[17] Hua Z, Jin F, Xu B, Huang H. 2d logistic-sine-coupling map for image encryption. Signal Processing. 2018;**149**: 148-161

[18] Wang X, Wang Y, Zhu X, Unar S. Image encryption scheme based on chaos and DNA plane operations. Multimedia Tools and Applications. 2019;**78**(18): 26111-26128

[19] Niu Y, Zhang X. An effective image encryption method based on space filling curve and plaintext-related Josephus traversal. IEEE Access. 2020;**8**: 196326-196340

[20] Niu Y, Zhou H, Zhang X, Qin L, et al. Hybrid encryption algorithm based on gray curve and Josephus permutation. Computational Intelligence and Neuroscience. 2022;**2022**:7076416

[21] Hénon M. A two-dimensional mapping with a strange attractor. In: The Theory of Chaotic Attractors. New York, NY: Springer; 1976. pp. 94-102

[22] Ibrahim S, Alharbi A. Efficient image encryption scheme using Henon map, dynamic s-boxes and elliptic curve cryptography. IEEE Access. 2020;**8**: 194289-194302

[23] Liu Y, Qin Z, Liao X, Wu J. A chaotic image encryption scheme based on Hénon–Chebyshev modulation map and genetic operations. International Journal of Bifurcation and Chaos. 2020;**30**(06): 2050090

[24] Mishra K, Saharan R. A fast image encryption technique using henon chaotic map. In: Progress in Advanced Computing and Intelligent Engineering. Singapore: Springer; 2019. pp. 329-339

[25] Chai Z, Liang S, Hu G, Zhang L, Wu Y, Cao C. Periodic characteristics of the Josephus ring and its application in image scrambling. EURASIP Journal on Wireless Communications and Networking. 2018;**2018**(1):1-11

[26] Halbeisen L, Hungerbühler N. The Josephus problem. Journal de Théorie des Nombres de Bordeaux. 1997;**9**(2): 303-318

[27] Schumer PD. Mathematical Journeys. Hoboken, New Jersey: John Wiley & Sons, Inc.; 2004

[28] Van Roy P, Haridi S. Concepts, Techniques, and Models of Computer Programming. Cambridge, Massachusetts London, England: The MIT Press; 2004

[29] Hua Z, Xu B, Jin F, Huang H. Image encryption using Josephus problem and filtering diffusion. IEEE Access. 2019;**7**: 8660-8674

[30] Zhang X, Wang L, Wang Y, Niu Y, Li Y. An image encryption algorithm based on hyperchaotic system and variable-step Josephus problem. International Journal of Optics. 2020; **2020**:1-15

[31] Kamal ST, Hosny KM, Elgindy TM, Darwish MM, Fouda MM. A new image encryption algorithm for grey and color medical images. IEEE Access. 2021;**9**: 37855-37865

[32] Ayubi P, Setayeshi S, Rahmani AM. Deterministic chaos game: A new fractal based pseudo-random number generator and its cryptographic application. Journal of Information Security and Applications. 2020;**52**:102472

[33] Iqbal N, Hanif M, Abbas S, Khan MA, Almotiri SH, Al Ghamdi MA. DNA strands level scrambling based color image encryption scheme. IEEE Access. 2020;**8**:178167-178182

[34] Hu X, Wei L, Chen W, Chen Q, Guo Y. Color image encryption algorithm based on dynamic chaos and matrix convolution. IEEE Access. 2020; **8**:12452-12466

[35] Hosny KM, Kamal ST, Darwish MM, Papakostas GA. New image encryption algorithm using hyperchaotic system and fibonacci q-matrix. Electronics. 2021; **10**(9):1066

[36] Murugan B, Nanjappa Gounder AG, Manohar S. A hybrid image encryption

algorithm using chaos and Conway's game-of-life cellular automata. Security and Communication Networks. 2016; **9**(7):634-651

[37] Zhang Y. The fast image encryption algorithm based on lifting scheme and chaos. Information Sciences. 2020;**520**: 177-194

Chapter 7

Perspective Chapter: Quantum Steganography – Encoding Secrets in the Quantum Domain

Arun Agrawal, Rishi Soni and Archana Tomar

Abstract

The chapter provides a comprehensive overview of the evolving field of quantum steganography, highlighting its potential impact on information security in the age of quantum computing. Steganography, rooted in ancient practices, has traditionally concealed data within classical computing systems, but the emergence of quantum computing poses new challenges. Quantum steganography adapts classical principles to leverage the unique properties of quantum mechanics, employing quantum bits (qubits), superposition, and entanglement for secure data concealment. The abstract delves into the conceptual framework of a quantum steganography algorithm, emphasizing its complexity and the integration of quantum key distribution for enhanced security. The applications span secure communication, medical records, financial transactions, military defense, intellectual property protection, and more. Despite promising prospects, quantum steganography faces challenges such as quantum state fragility and hardware constraints, requiring ongoing research to unlock its full potential in safeguarding sensitive information.

Keywords: quantum steganography, quantum computing, qubits, superposition, entanglement

1. Introduction

In the rapidly evolving landscape of digital communication and data security, one field has long remained instrumental in the concealment and safeguarding of sensitive information: steganography [1]. This artful practice, originating from the ancient Greeks who used it for hiding secret messages, revolves around embedding data within seemingly unremarkable files or transmissions to obfuscate their true nature. Steganography is a potent tool for ensuring the confidentiality and integrity of data in various contexts, such as protecting intellectual property, confidential government documents, and personal information [2].

Traditionally, steganography has been confined to the realm of classical computing and communication systems. Its techniques have been predominantly applied to hide information within images, audio files, or text [3]. The modus operandi of classical steganography involves making subtle modifications to the host data that are imperceptible to the human eye or ear. While these techniques have been effective in securing data from casual eavesdroppers or attackers, they are not immune to advanced cryptanalysis methods.

The emergence of quantum computing and quantum information theory has opened up new horizons for steganography [4]. Quantum computing, with its revolutionary processing power and cryptographic implications, introduces an intriguing challenge and opportunity for data security [5]. In this quantum frontier, quantum steganography is born.

Quantum steganography adapts the principles of classical steganography to the unique properties of quantum systems [6]. In the quantum realm, information can exist in superposition and become entangled, allowing for novel ways to hide and retrieve data. Quantum steganography leverages these quantum phenomena to encode information within quantum states, making it potentially more secure and robust against quantum adversaries who possess powerful quantum computers [7].

In the field of quantum steganography, the basic principles revolve around using qubits as transmitters of hidden information. By cleverly manipulating the inherent quantum state of a qubit, information is embedded in a way that is particularly difficult to detect or decipher. Quantum steganography adds another layer of security by exploiting the phenomenon of quantum entanglement, in which the properties of one qubit depend on the state of another qubit. Modifications of the state of entangled qubits facilitate data encoding; any effort to intercept or manipulate the information destroys this delicate entanglement. This disruption is a clear indicator of intrusion and enhances the security of hidden information in the complex field of quantum steganography [8].

The potential avenues for quantum steganography are vast and promising. Especially in the field of quantum communications, it has the potential to improve the security of quantum key distribution protocols and ensure the confidentiality of keys exchanged between entities. Furthermore, the field of quantum steganography extends its scope of protection to sensitive data stored in quantum databases or transmitted through quantum channels [9]. This versatility makes it a powerful defense against a range of threats, whether classical or emerging from the quantum realm. Quantum steganography has become a powerful guardian with its many applications, ushering in a new era of security in the field of complex quantum communication and data transmission.

Despite its potential, practical applications of quantum steganography are still in the early stages of development. Researchers are actively studying the complexities, limitations, and best practices associated with quantum steganography. Challenges such as noise in quantum systems, the urgent need for error correction, and the development of effective detection methods for quantum steganographic payloads constitute obstacles that need to be thoroughly explored and addressed in this emerging field [10].

2. Understanding steganography

Steganography as a concept has a rich history that predates the digital era. This includes techniques that hide information or messages behind a seemingly innocuous cover, such as a physical object, text, or even a digital file. This technique has been employed by individuals and organizations for centuries to protect sensitive information and communicate discreetly while avoiding prying eyes and potential adversaries. With the dawn of the digital era, steganography seamlessly transitioned into the realm of digital data, paving the way for the development of classic steganography techniques [11].

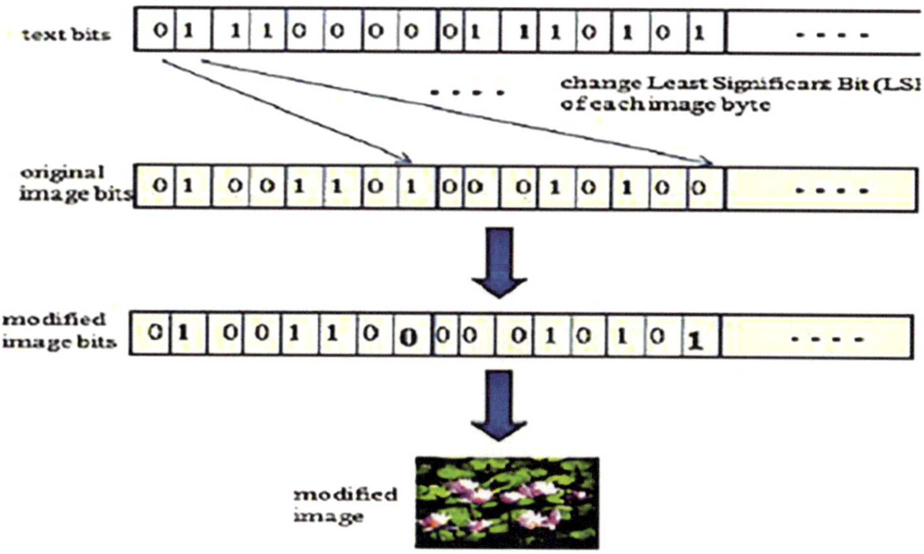

Figure 1.
Inserting the text bits into the image.

Classic steganography in digital form revolves around the concept of embedding data within a host medium such as an image, audio file, or text. One of the most common methods used in this field is to manipulate the least significant bits of digital files [12]. For example, in an image, the color of individual pixels can be slightly changed to encode hidden information as shown in **Figure 1**. The human eye typically cannot discern these subtle changes, making it a suitable medium for secret data transmission.

In audio files, the least significant bits of an audio sample can be adjusted to convey hidden data that is similarly indiscernible to the human ear. Text files can also be used for steganographic purposes, allowing hidden messages to be hidden within the text itself or by using certain encoding techniques as shown in **Figure 2**.

Classic steganography is widely used for a variety of purposes, including protecting intellectual property, sensitive government documents, and confidential communications [11]. However, they are not immune to detection and decryption efforts, and rapid

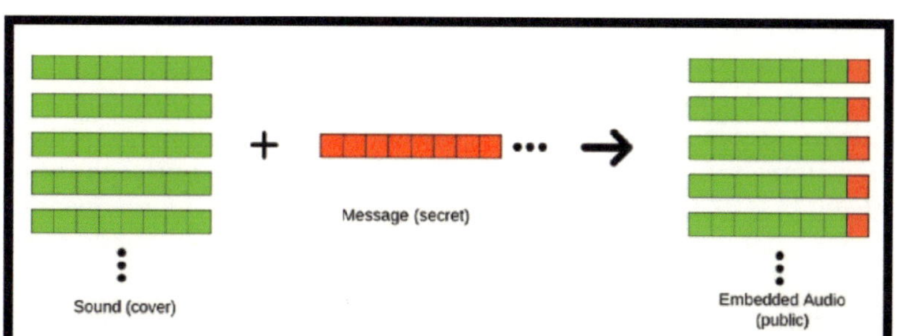

Figure 2.
Embedding secret message in audio.

advances in computing power and algorithms are making it increasingly difficult to ensure the security of information hidden in classical steganography systems.

The advent of quantum computing ushered in a new era, bringing new challenges and exciting opportunities to the field of steganography. Quantum computing, with its unparalleled processing power, threatens traditional encryption methods and offers the potential to more easily crack steganography systems. However, it also provides a unique platform for quantum steganography to evolve and flourish.

In the field of quantum information security, quantum steganography cleverly adapts the principles of classical steganography to the complex realm of quantum systems. This innovative approach takes advantage of the unique properties of quantum bits (qubits) to hide information in a way that goes beyond the scope of classical steganography. Unlike its classical counterpart, quantum steganography exploits the concept of superposition, allowing qubits to exist in multiple states simultaneously [13]. This is an ideal feature for secret embedding of data. Furthermore, an additional layer of security is added by incorporating quantum entanglement, a phenomenon in which the states of interconnected qubits intertwine [14]. Any attempt to intercept information disrupts this complex entanglement and increases the protection of data hidden within the delicate context of quantum steganography.

3. Quantum steganography: principles and techniques

Quantum steganography is at the forefront of secure communications and data hiding, leveraging the unique principles of quantum mechanics to encode and hide information in a way that classical steganography cannot replicate. At its core, quantum steganography relies on three fundamental concepts: quantum superposition, quantum entanglement, and quantum key distribution (QKD) [15]. Each of these principles plays a vital role in ensuring the security and integrity of information transmitted in the complex realm of quantum mechanics.

The concept of quantum superposition is a cornerstone of quantum mechanics and provides unique advantages in the field of quantum steganography [16]. In classical computing, bits are limited to existing as either 0 or 1. However, due to the phenomenon of quantum superposition, qubits, or qubits, can exist in multiple states at the same time. This property allows expert manipulation of quantum states, enabling the embedding of hidden information in qubits [17]. The information remains hidden until it is accurately measured, at which point the qubit collapses into one of its potential states, specifically revealing the hidden data to the intended recipient. This inherent property makes quantum steganography exceptionally secure, as it poses a significant challenge to unauthorized entities attempting to intercept or decrypt without the necessary measurement and decryption technology [18].

Quantum entanglement is another fascinating phenomenon in quantum mechanics that adds an extra layer of security to quantum steganography. This property involves the interconnection of two or more qubits, regardless of the physical distance between them. In the context of quantum steganography, this interconnection creates a level of connection between sender and receiver that is highly resistant to destruction or tampering by eavesdroppers. Any attempt to intercept the communication will destroy the subtle entanglement and become an obvious sign of intrusion. Quantum entanglement therefore provides a unique form of security beyond classical encryption methods, making quantum steganography a promising avenue to facilitate secure communication and discreet hiding of information [19].

Quantum Key Distribution (QKD) emerged as an important component of quantum steganography, operating on the principles of quantum mechanics within the broader field of quantum cryptography. QKD facilitates the secure exchange of encryption keys between senders and receivers and is the cornerstone of establishing secure communication channels. The use of quantum encryption keys allows mutual authentication between communicating parties, thereby creating an enhanced environment for the exchange of steganographic information [20]. Notably, QKD ensures that the key exchange is interception-proof, as any eavesdropping attempt will destroy the quantum properties of the key, thus promptly alerting interested parties of a potential security breach. The combination of QKD therefore adds an additional layer of security, making quantum steganography a reliable method of protecting sensitive information [21].

Essentially, quantum steganography exploits the unique properties of quantum superposition, quantum entanglement, and QKD to provide an extremely secure method of encoding and hiding information within quantum states. Together, these quantum properties provide unparalleled security, making it extremely challenging for unauthorized parties to intercept, decipher, or tamper with hidden data. As we enter the era of quantum computing and traditional encryption methods face increasing vulnerabilities, quantum steganography emerges as an innovative and promising method to ensure the confidentiality and integrity of sensitive information.

The complex dance of quantum superposition allows for the secret embedding of information in quantum states, while the strong security provided by quantum entanglement creates a communication channel that is highly resistant to external interference. Using QKD as a basis ensures the secure exchange of encryption keys, further enhancing the overall security of quantum steganography. As a result, quantum steganography becomes a powerful tool in the field of secure communication and data hiding, paving the way for new possibilities in the evolving field of quantum information processing.

4. Conceptual framework for a quantum steganography algorithm

Designing a specific quantum steganography algorithm involves intricate quantum operations and encoding techniques to hide data within quantum states [22, 23]. Below, a simplified conceptual algorithm to give an idea of how quantum steganography might work is shown in **Figure 3**:

- *Initialization*: Generate two entangled qubits: Qubit_A and Qubit_B, such that their states are correlated. Prepare Qubit_A in a superposition state that will represent the hidden information. The specific state preparation depends on the encoding method chosen.

- *Encoding*: Embed the data you want to hide in the quantum superposition of Qubit_A. The exact encoding method will depend on the chosen strategy. For example, you might perform quantum gates, phase shifts, or other quantum operations to represent the hidden information within the superposition.

- *Transmission*: Share Qubit_B, which remains entangled with Qubit_A, with the intended receiver through a secure quantum communication channel.

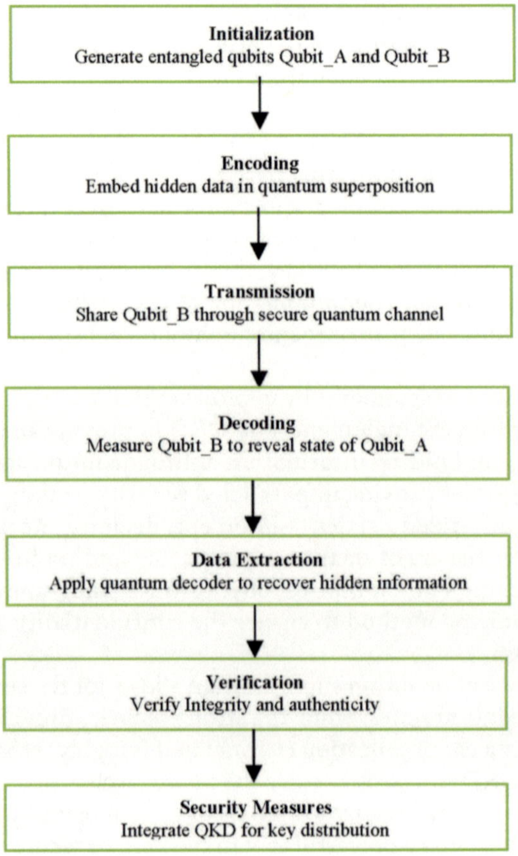

Figure 3.
Flowchart of simplified conceptual algorithm.

- *Decoding*: The receiver measures Qubit_B. This measurement can reveal the state of Qubit_A due to their entanglement.

- *Data extraction*: Apply a quantum decoder to recover the hidden information from the state of Qubit_A. The decoder should understand the encoding method used in the encoding step.

- *Verification*: Verify the integrity and authenticity of the received data, ensuring it has not been tampered with during transmission. This can be done through error-checking codes or other cryptographic methods.

- *Security measures*: Enhance the security of the quantum steganography process by integrating quantum key distribution (QKD) protocols to protect the encryption keys used for encoding and decoding. This ensures that the keys remain secret and unobservable to potential eavesdroppers.

It's essential to note that this is a simplified conceptual overview of a quantum steganography algorithm. In practice, the details can become significantly more complex, and the choice of encoding and decoding methods, as well as the integration of quantum cryptographic protocols, will depend on the specific requirements and security considerations of the application. Quantum steganography is still an emerging field, and ongoing research is exploring more advanced techniques and practical implementations.

5. Simulators used in quantum steganography

A Quantum Steganography simulator combines quantum computing, secrecy, and simulation, allowing users to explore the fusion of quantum principles with covert communication. This innovative tool facilitates the understanding and experimentation of hiding information within quantum states. By blending elements of quantum mechanics with steganographic techniques, the simulator provides a virtual environment for studying the security implications and applications of quantum-secured communication [24]. Here are some Simulators:

- QuantumSecSim
- StegaSimQ
- CryptoQuantaSim
- QubitConceal
- SimuSecQuant
- EnigmaQuantSim
- QuantumCloakSim
- SimuCryptQuant
- StealthQuantSim
- CipherQuantumSim

Here, we discuss about the environment of QuantumSecSim simulator [25].

The QuantumSecSim simulator environment is a cutting-edge platform that combines the fields of quantum computing, cryptography, and steganography to provide comprehensive tools for understanding and exploring secure communications in the quantum world. The simulator is designed to provide users with an interactive and educational experience that allows them to delve into the complexities of quantum secure communications and quantum steganography.

- *Quantum computing simulation*: At the heart of QuantumSecSim is a powerful quantum computing simulation module. Users can experiment with quantum bits (qubits), quantum gates, and build complex quantum circuits [26]. The simulator provides a realistic environment for simulating quantum operations and algorithms, allowing users to gain practical experience with quantum principles.

- *Cryptography module*: QuantumSecSim contains dedicated cryptographic modules emphasizing the Quantum Key Distribution (QKD) protocol. Users can simulate and analyze the behavior of the QKD algorithm, which is the cornerstone of secure communications in the quantum realm. The module also introduces users to quantum-safe cryptography to prepare them for the post-quantum era [27].

- *Steganography features*: The simulator pushes the boundaries by integrating steganography technology that exploits quantum properties. Users can explore how quantum states and their unique capabilities, such as superposition and entanglement, can be exploited to securely hide classical information. QuantumSecSim provides a canvas for experimenting with various quantum steganography methods and understanding their applications in hiding quantum state information [28].

- *Security analysis tools*: Understanding the robustness and vulnerability of quantum-safe communications is critical. QuantumSecSim provides users with advanced security analysis tools for evaluating the ability of quantum steganography methods to withstand potential attacks [29]. Users can explore different threat scenarios, helping them gain insights into the strengths and weaknesses of quantum security systems.

- *User interface (UI)*: The simulator has an intuitive and user-friendly interface, ensuring that both beginners and experienced users can use it. The UI facilitates the creation, execution, and analysis of simulations. Visual tools help users understand complex quantum states, encryption protocols, and steganographic processes [30], thereby enhancing the overall learning experience.

- *Educational resources*: To support users on their quantum journey, QuantumSecSim offers a wide range of educational resources. It includes tutorials, documentation, and example scenarios to guide users through basic concepts and practical applications [31]. The purpose of this simulator is not only to simulate quantum phenomena, but also to educate and empower users in the quantum realm.

- *Customization and extensibility*: Recognizing the dynamic nature of quantum technology, QuantumSecSim is designed to be customizable and scalable. Users can customize simulation parameters to suit specific scenarios and experiment with emerging quantum algorithms, encryption protocols, and steganography techniques. The platform's adaptability ensures it remains at the forefront of quantum research and development.

- *Simulation output and analysis*: QuantumSecSim provides detailed output and analysis tools that enable users to effectively interpret simulation results. Users can evaluate the performance, security, and efficiency of quantum secure communication methods to gain a deeper understanding of the impact and potential applications of quantum steganography.

The QuantumSecSim simulator environment serves as a gateway to the quantum-secured future, offering an immersive and educational experience. By seamlessly integrating quantum computing, cryptography, and steganography, QuantumSecSim empowers users to unlock the secrets of secure communication in the quantum era. This innovative platform not only simulates quantum phenomena but also educates and inspires the next generation of quantum enthusiasts and researchers.

6. Applications of quantum steganography

Quantum steganography is an emerging field with diverse applications in the realm of secure communication and data protection. Here are ten potential applications of quantum steganography:

- *Secure communication*: Quantum steganography can provide a highly secure means of communication, where sensitive information is hidden within quantum states, making it extremely difficult for unauthorized parties to intercept or decipher the data [32].

- *Quantum key distribution (QKD)*: Quantum steganography can enhance QKD by concealing cryptographic keys within quantum states. This ensures that the keys remain secret and protected from eavesdroppers, bolstering the security of quantum communication [33].

- *Quantum internet*: As the development of quantum internet progresses, quantum steganography can be used to secure data transmission and communication over long-distance quantum networks [34].

- *Medical records*: Concealing sensitive patient data within quantum states can enhance the privacy and security of electronic health records, protecting personal information from unauthorized access [35].

- *Financial transactions*: Quantum steganography can be applied to secure financial transactions and data, making it more difficult for cybercriminals to intercept or manipulate sensitive financial information [32].

- *Military and defense*: Quantum steganography can be employed for secure communication within military and defense organizations, protecting classified information from adversaries [36].

- *Intellectual property protection*: Companies can use quantum steganography to protect their intellectual property by concealing critical data within quantum states, reducing the risk of industrial espionage [32].

- *Secure cloud storage*: Quantum steganography can be applied to encrypt and hide data stored in the cloud, adding an extra layer of security to cloud-based storage solutions [36].

- *Government communications*: Government agencies can use quantum steganography to secure classified and sensitive communications, safeguarding national security interests [37].

- *Protecting sensitive research*: Researchers working on cutting-edge scientific projects can employ quantum steganography to secure their findings and intellectual property, preventing unauthorized access or theft [32, 35].
- *Smart grid security*: In the context of the smart grid, quantum steganography can help protect critical infrastructure and ensure secure communication within the energy distribution network, reducing the risk of cyberattacks [36].
- *Supply chain security*: Quantum steganography can be applied to secure information related to the supply chain, ensuring the confidentiality and integrity of data, such as shipping schedules and product designs [13, 22, 29].
- *Law enforcement and criminal investigations*: Law enforcement agencies can use quantum steganography to safeguard sensitive investigative information and protect the identities of undercover officers and informants [38].
- *Secure voting systems*: Quantum steganography can enhance the security of electronic voting systems by concealing and protecting voter data, making it more resistant to tampering or hacking [39].
- *Blockchain security*: Quantum steganography can bolster the security of blockchain technology by concealing private keys and transaction details, safeguarding cryptocurrency assets and transaction history [35].

These applications highlight the potential of quantum steganography to address various security and privacy challenges in the modern world, making it a valuable tool for securing information in the quantum age.

7. Challenges and future prospects

Quantum steganography is an emerging field in information security that is grappling with the challenges of standing out in the world of covert communications. The main obstacle is the fragility of quantum states, which are highly susceptible to external disturbances. Unlike traditional steganography, which hides information in classical bits of data, quantum steganography operates in the complex quantum realm and requires nuanced hiding methods [40].

One of the unique challenges of quantum steganography comes from the fragility of quantum states. Quantum superposition is a key concept in quantum mechanics, which allows quantum particles to exist in multiple states at the same time. While this property facilitates the encoding of hidden information within quantum states, it also makes these states highly sensitive. External interference or measurements may corrupt the superposition, potentially revealing hidden information. This delicate balance poses the challenge of designing robust quantum steganography techniques that can withstand potential interference and ensure secure transmission of information.

Unlike classical steganography, which hides information within classical data bits, quantum steganography operates according to the principles of quantum mechanics. This shift introduces a paradigm where the rules of classical information hiding do not directly apply. The challenge is to develop methods that exploit the unique properties of quantum mechanics to effectively hide information. As mentioned earlier, quantum superposition and entanglement become critical in this endeavor, allowing the creation of secure communication channels and hiding information that is inherently resistant to unauthorized access.

Additionally, the infancy of quantum computing technology adds additional complexity to the implementation of quantum steganography. Successful execution requires advanced quantum hardware and precise error correction mechanisms. Theoretical concepts must be seamlessly integrated with practical hardware constraints, highlighting the complex interplay between the theoretical foundations of quantum steganography and the capabilities of emerging quantum technologies [16].

To illustrate this point, consider the application of quantum steganography in quantum key distribution (QKD). QKD leverages the principles of quantum mechanics to enable secure communication by exchanging quantum keys between the sender and receiver. Quantum steganography can enhance the security of QKD by hiding information within the quantum states exchanged during key distribution. This additional hidden layer ensures that even if an adversary intercepts the quantum key exchange, deciphering the hidden information remains a difficult challenge.

Despite these challenges, the potential of quantum steganography to enhance information security remains promising. Researchers and experts actively explore this uncharted territory, developing applications, describing limitations, and refining strategies to improve efficiency and reliability. As quantum technology matures, the unique capabilities of quantum steganography may lead to novel solutions for protecting sensitive information.

Quantum steganography represents an emerging frontier in information security, characterized by the unique challenges posed by the delicate nature of quantum states and the nascent stages of quantum computing technology. While these challenges are significant, they also highlight the uniqueness of quantum steganography in protecting information in ways that classical methods cannot achieve. As researchers continue to explore this complex field, the potential of quantum steganography to revolutionize secure communications remains promising, marking a unique chapter in the evolution of information security.

8. Conclusion

Quantum steganography, a cutting-edge realm in information security, utilizes the distinctive features of quantum mechanics to revolutionize digital communication and data storage security in the era of quantum computing. Unlike classical steganography, which hides information in plain sight, quantum steganography leverages quantum entanglement and superposition to encode data in quantum states, making it exceptionally resistant to unauthorized interception or decryption.

As quantum technologies progress, the role of quantum steganography is poised to expand, offering unparalleled protection for sensitive information. Its capacity to operate within the quantum realm aligns with the escalating demand for robust data security measures. In the evolving landscape of information protection, quantum steganography emerges as a promising safeguard, ensuring confidentiality and integrity amidst the increasing challenges posed by sophisticated cyber threats and the impending era of quantum computing.

Author details

Arun Agrawal*, Rishi Soni and Archana Tomar
Department of Computer Science and Engineering, Institute of Technology and Management, Gwalior, India

*Address all correspondence to: arun.agarwal@itmgoi.in

References

[1] Danezis G, Domingo-Ferrer J, Hansen M, Hoepman J-H, Le Metayer D, Tirtea R, et al. Privacy and data protection by design: From policy to engineering (report). Retrieved from the Publications Office of the European Union Website. 2014. DOI: 10.2824/38623

[2] Mawla NA, Khafaji HK. Enhancing data security: A cutting-edge approach utilizing protein chains in cryptography and steganography. Computers. 2023;**12**(8):166

[3] Sinha N, Bhowmick A, Kishore B. Encrypted information hiding using audio steganography and audio cryptography. International Journal of Computer Applications. 2015;**112**(5):49-53

[4] Pathak A. Elements of Quantum Computation and Quantum Communication. Boca Raton, FL: CRC Press, Taylor & Francis Group; 2013

[5] Li S, Chen Y, Chen L, Liao J, Kuang C, Li K, et al. Post-quantum security: Opportunities and challenges. Sensors. 2023;**23**(21):8744

[6] Chaharlang J, Mosleh M, Rasouli-Heikalabad S. A novel quantum steganography-steganalysis system for audio signals. Multimedia Tools and Applications. 2020;**79**(25-26):17551-17577

[7] Krenn M, Malik M, Scheidl T, Ursin R, Zeilinger A. Quantum communication with photons. Optics in Our Time. 2016;**18**:455

[8] Singh S, Bharathi V. Quantum cryptography research over the past two decades–review, research implications, and future directions. In: AIP Conference Proceedings. Vol. 2869, No. 1. AIP Publishing; 2023. pp. 106-119

[9] Maurya S, Nandu N, Patel T, Reddy VD, Tiwari S, Morampudi MK. A discrete cosine transform-based intelligent image steganography scheme using quantum substitution box. Quantum Information Processing. 2023;**22**(5):206

[10] Qu Z, Huang Y, Zheng M. A novel coherence-based quantum steganalysis protocol. Quantum Information Processing. 2020;**19**:1-19

[11] Wayner P. Disappearing Cryptography: Information Hiding: Steganography and Watermarking. 3rd ed. Boston, MA: Morgan Kaufmann; 2009

[12] Artz D. Digital steganography: Hiding data within data. IEEE Internet Computing. 2001;**5**(3):75-80

[13] Moyou Metcheka L, Ndoundam R. Distributed data hiding in multi-cloud storage environment. Journal of Cloud Computing. 2020;**9**(1):68

[14] Awschalom D, Berggren KK, Bernien H, Bhave S, Carr LD, Davids P, et al. Development of quantum interconnects (quics) for next-generation information technologies. PRX Quantum. 2021;**2**(1):017002

[15] Tudorache AG, Manta V, Caraiman S. Quantum steganography based on the B92 quantum protocol. Mathematics. 2022;**10**(16):2870

[16] Shaw BA. Quantum Steganography and Quantum Error-Correction [Doctoral dissertation]. University of Southern California, USC Digital Library; 2010

[17] Ruan S, Yuan R, Guan Q, Lin Y, Mao Y, Jiang W, et al. Venus: A geometrical representation for quantum state visualization. Computer Graphics Forum. 2023;**42**(3):247-258

[18] Gea-Banacloche J. Hiding messages in quantum data. Journal of Mathematical Physics. 2002;**43**(9):4531-4536

[19] Mihara T. Quantum steganography using prior entanglement. Physics Letters A. 2015;**379**(12-13):952-955

[20] Kumar A, Garhwal S. State-of-the-art survey of quantum cryptography. Archives of Computational Methods in Engineering. 2021;**28**:3831-3868

[21] Alléaume R, Branciard C, Bouda J, Debuisschert T, Dianati M, Gisin N, et al. Using quantum key distribution for cryptographic purposes: A survey. Theoretical Computer Science. 2014;**560**:62-81

[22] Bahaddad AA, Almarhabi KA, Abdel-Khalek S. Image steganography technique based on bald eagle search optimal pixel selection with chaotic encryption. Alexandria Engineering Journal. 2023;**75**:41-54

[23] Harun NZ, Ahmad Zukarnain Z, Hanapi ZM, Ahmad I. Multi-stage quantum secure direct communication using secure shared authentication key. Symmetry. 2020;**12**(9):1481

[24] Ur Rasool R, Ahmad HF, Rafique W, Qayyum A, Qadir J, Anwar Z. Quantum computing for healthcare: A review. Future Internet. 2023;**15**(3):94

[25] Giraldo-Carvajal A, Jaramillo-Villegas JA. QuantumSkynet: A high dimensional quantum computing simulator. In: Laser Science (JW6A.25). Optica Publishing Group; 2020. DOI: 10.1364/LS.2020.JW6A.25

[26] Georgopoulos K, Emary C, Zuliani P. Quantum computer benchmarking via quantum algorithms. 2021. ArXiv, art. 2112.09457v1. Available from: https://arxiv.org/pdf/2112.09457.pdf [Accessed: September 20, 2023]

[27] Dragone S. How We Quantum-Proofed IBM z16. IBM Research Blog; 11 October 2022. Available from: https://research.ibm.com/blog/z16-quantum-safe-migration

[28] Min-Allah N, Nagy N, Aljabri M, Alkharraa M, Alqahtani M, Alghamdi D, et al. Quantum image steganography schemes for data hiding: A survey. Applied Sciences. 2022;**12**(20):10294

[29] Abd-El-Atty B, Iliyasu AM, Alaskar H, Abd El-Latif AA. A robust quasi-quantum walks-based steganography protocol for secure transmission of images on cloud-based E-healthcare platforms. Sensors. 2020;**20**(11):3108

[30] Sathananthavathi V, Ganesh Kumar K, Sathish Kumar M. Secure visual communication with advanced cryptographic and image processing techniques. Multimedia Tools and Applications. 2023;**82**:1-23. DOI: 10.1007/s11042-023-14481-8

[31] Paudel HP, Syamlal M, Crawford SE, Lee YL, Shugayev RA, Lu P, et al. Quantum computing and simulations for energy applications: Review and perspective. ACS Engineering Au. 2022;**2**(3):151-196

[32] Kumar M, Gupta A, Shah K, Saurabh A, Saxena P, Tiwari VK. Data security using Stegnography and quantum cryptography. Network and Complex Systems. 2012;**2**(2):46-55

[33] Sasikumar S, Sundar K, Jayakumar C, Obaidat MS, Stephan T, Hsiao KF. Modeling and simulation of a novel

secure quantum key distribution (SQKD) for ensuring data security in cloud environment. Simulation Modelling Practice and Theory. 2022;**121**:102651

[34] Rozenman GG, Kundu NK, Liu R, Zhang L, Maslennikov A, Reches Y, et al. The quantum internet: A synergy of quantum information technologies and 6G networks. IET Quantum Communication. 2023;**4**(4):147-166

[35] Qu Z, Zhang Z, Zheng M. A quantum blockchain-enabled framework for secure private electronic medical records in internet of medical things. Information Sciences. 2022;**612**:942-958

[36] Ralegankar VK, Bagul J, Thakkar B, Gupta R, Tanwar S, Sharma G, et al. Quantum cryptography-as-a-service for secure UAV communication: Applications, challenges, and case study. IEEE Access. 2021;**10**:1475-1492

[37] Patil BP, Kharade KG, Kharade SK, Kamat RK. Significant study of data encryption and steganography. Recent Advances in Mathematical Research and Computer Science. 2021;**1**:79-91

[38] Aguirre B. Steganography in contemporary cyberattacks and the link to child pornography [Doctoral dissertation]. Utica College, Utica College Library; 2020

[39] Junior Gabriel A, Alese BK, Adetunmbi AO, Adewale OS, Sarumi OA. Post-quantum crystography system for secure electronic voting. Open Computer Science. 2019;**9**(1):292-298

[40] Laishram D, Tuithung T. A survey on digital image steganography: Current trends and challenges. In: Proceedings of 3rd International Conference on Internet of Things and Connected Technologies (ICIoTCT). Jaipur, India: Malaviya National Institute of Technology; 26-27 March 2018. pp. 26-27

Chapter 8

Network Covert Channels

Muawia Elsadig

Abstract

With the rapid advancement of communication and computer network technologies, covert channels are now more secure, quicker to set up, harder to detect, and easier to design than ever before. By breaking a system security policy, a covert channel can be utilized to leak confidential communications. Undoubtedly, one of the most difficult challenges is still detecting such harmful, unobservable, and covert dangers. Due to the fact that this danger takes advantage of techniques not intended for communication, it is invisible to conventional security solutions. This chapter offers a concise overview of covert channel concept, techniques, classifications, and countermeasures, emphasizing how new technologies are vulnerable to being exploited for initiation of different covert channels and how they offer a rich environment for developing effective but challenging covert channel attacks. It gives a comprehensive review of common covert channel countermeasures with more focus on machine learning detection techniques. Although some research studies have revealed beneficial uses of covert channel, which is natural given that many approaches have a double-edged sword impact, this chapter focuses on covert channels as a security threat that compromise our data and networks.

Keywords: covert channel, network covert channel, data hiding, information security, network security, cybersecurity, machine learning, security, covert storage channel, steganography, covert timing channel

1. Introduction

A communication channel between two parties (sender and recipient) that are not permitted to exchange information is known as a covert channel [1]. A significant area of study in information concealment is covert communication, which uses hidden routes to send information covertly. When people are communicating covertly, their relationship can be safeguarded and confidential information cannot be reached, detected, or recovered by unauthorized parties [2]. On the other hand, a covert channel provides an open avenue for hackers to spread destructive activity or leak private information without being discovered [3].

Attackers are increasingly using steganographic and information-hiding tactics to evade detection and stay undetected for extended periods of time. They have, for example, been used to exfiltrate secret information in Advanced Persistent Threats (APTs), conceal the presence of malware within seemingly innocent images, and conceal malicious code or extra functionalities with the goal of implementing covert multistage loading architectures. Creating covert channels is one of the most common and successful techniques of information concealment to promote insecurity [4].

The expansion of computer networks and intrusion detection systems has given rise to creative methods by which hackers might pilfer or reveal sensitive data. A network hidden channel or covert channel may be used to do this, which is a useful bonus.

With a covert channel, people may share secret information while being invisible to one another. In addition to being used for the transmission of secret information, covert channels may also be used to transmit malware, Trojan horses, viruses, and other threats in a fashion that evades detection by standard firewalls or detection programs. When such harmful acts are paired with a covert channel, the combination is considered a major threat.

Cabaj et al. stated that fraudsters have employed a variety of information-hiding strategies with evil intent. Among other possible techniques, attackers are increasingly using network covert channels to mask their harmful activity, such as downloading more malware modules or exfiltrating sensitive and private data. It should be noted that this trend is anticipated to continue, and the digital forensics and security industries will face significant challenges as there is a rise in the use of advanced covert channel techniques for harmful purposes [5]. Cabaj et al. further stated that in order to facilitate hidden data exchange, attackers can use Distributed Network Covert Channels (DNCCs), which are defined as network covert channels that disperse secret data among numerous flows, protocols, and hosts or that employ a variety of data hiding methods within a single flow or within Protocol Data Units (PDUs). The security industry is paying more attention to DNCCs these days since they give the attacker the following advantages: (i) they allow sending of smaller parts of secret data *via* a variety of covert channels, which can increase the overall stealth and bandwidth of the concealed connection, and (ii) they enable getting beyond protective measures that are already in place, which make it harder to detect these types of covert channels.

Steganographic material was previously communicated using invisible ink or concealed tattoos. These days, steganography may be easily communicated with thanks to computer and network technology. The military, intelligence operations, and online social networks can all benefit from the usage of covert channels to ensure user privacy or coordinate protests and so on [6].

In certain situations, a covert channel can be used to conceal secret messages rather than posing a threat. For example, a network administrator may utilize a covert channel to safeguard network management communications from hacker assaults. In addition, for several security techniques, like copyright protection, network authentication, cybercrime evidence, and so forth, covert channel technology has emerged as a cutting-edge technique [7]. Although many research studies have revealed beneficial uses of covert channels [8–10], they pose real security challenge and risks.

This section provides an overview, definitions, and important concerns related to the idea of covert channels. Furthermore, it emphasizes that covert channels are not always dangerous; in fact, their technology may be used for security objectives, as copyright defense, network authentication, cybercrime evidence, and other security strategies have found new applications for covert channels. The remaining part of the chapter is presented as follows: Section 2 divides covert channels into two categories, one classifies covert channels into two classes, covert storage channels and covert timing channels, while the second classifies them in three classifications: host-based, network-based, and physical. Subsequently, Section 3 addresses network covert channel classification. The typical covert channel model is illustrated in Section 4.

Section 5 outlines some factors that are behind the advanced development of covert channels and have direct impact in their widespread, while Section 6 discusses the prevalent of covert channel techniques in modern technologies and how they may offer a rich environment for creating many scenarios of covert communication that can have both beneficial and detrimental effects. Section 7 illustrates the countermeasures that are commonly used to counter covert channel, while Section 8 gives through and comprehensive details on covert channel identification methods with a focus on their achievements and drawbacks. A discussion and recommendations are provided in Section 9, while the chapter is concluded in Section 10.

2. Type of covert channels

A communication channel used to leak confidential information in a manner that is against security policy of a system is known as a covert channel. It is a highly hazardous, undetectable, persistent, and evolving threat that eludes detection technologies and presents a real challenge [11]. The idea of a covert channel was initially presented by Lampson [12]. Basically, covert channels can be classified into two types: covert timing channels and covert storage channels [13]. A method that lets one process to write to a shared storage location and permits another process to read from that storage location is considered a covert storage channel [14]. Both the read and write processes might run on a single computer setting or on a networked system. The operations of encoding secret information into network protocol fields (sender) and receiving the information back (receiver) are referred to as network covert storage channels. Two methods may be used to achieve it: the first modifies packet header information (such Internet Protocol ID, Time to live (TTL), and Type of Service (ToS)); the second modifies the length of the packet. In covert timing channels, a sender conveys secret data through the manipulation of packets, frames, or message timing; the intended recipient can then observe and decode the covert data. Covert timing channels also can exist in a networked or single-machine environment [13].

This categorization makes two configurations for a covert channel possible: a networked system and a stand-alone system. The secret data is sent between entities in the stand-alone system, whereas the secret data is sent *via* the network in a system that is network-based [15]. The research community first concentrated on what are known as local covert channels, which allow two processes with varying security levels to communicate to each other and exchange data. A process with a high security level usually divulges information to a process with a low security level. The emphasis has switched to network covert channels, where covert data may be encoded into a network protocol, as a result of the emergence and quick growth of computer networks [16].

Miketic et al. [1] indicated that host-based, network-based, and physical are the three basic categories into which covert channels fall. The timing and storage characteristics of the host system are usually altered in host-based covert channels. Network-based covert channels allow devices connected to a network to communicate with each other by modifying a portion of the network traffic. Lastly, using physical sources or side-channel signals (such as power, temperature, electromagnetic radiation, or optical) to transmit and encode data is known as physical covert channel. To ensure a dependable communication channel, physical covert channels need a certain level of closeness between the transmitter and receiver components. **Figure 1** shows the aforementioned three types of covert channel, which include host-based, network-based, and physical covert channels.

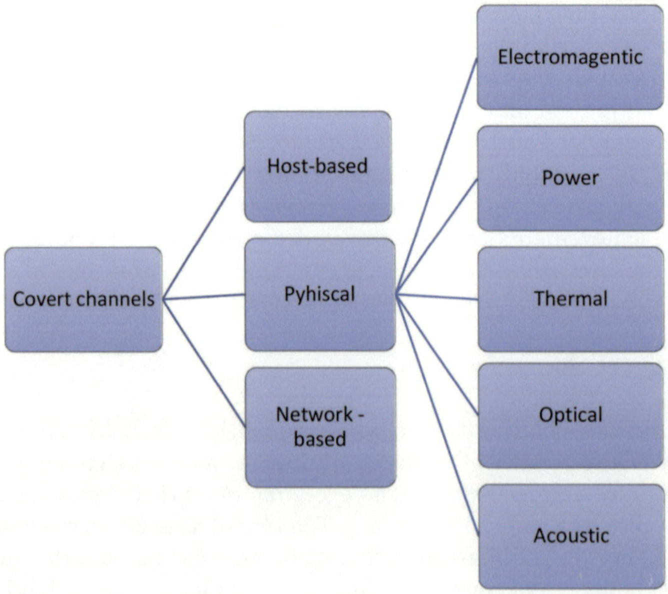

Figure 1.
Covert channel types [1].

3. Network covert channel classification

Network covert channels are information exchange channels that let two processes on the network to connect in a way that is beyond the system's security guidelines. In 1987, Grilling expanded the idea of a covert channel to include networked computer settings. In a local area network, Grilling created the first network covert channel. Hackers and steganographers have been inspired to create various network covert channel scenarios by the quick evolution of network protocols and methods. This has led to the development of several network-based covert channel approaches [17].

Network covert channels are often classified into two types: network covert timing channels and network covert storage channels [18, 19].

Encoding covert data into network protocol fields by a sender and receiving it back by a receiver are the two activities that make up a network covert storage channel. Through adjusting packets, frames, or message timing, a sender can transmit secret information and the intended recipient can then watch and decode the concealed data. These two activates of the sender and recipient make up a network covert timing channel. Network covert timing channels may be used maliciously to spread malware, plan attacks, and steal secrets, all of which pose major risks to cybersecurity [20].

Two methods are available to achieve network covert storage channels: the first modifies packet header information (such Internet Protocol ID, Time to live (TTL), and Type of Service (ToS)); the second modifies packet length. It is evident that network covert storage channels have a substantially larger bandwidth than the covert timing channels. As a result, network covert storage channels have drawn greater attention than their time channels. They pose a severe risk and have the potential to cause major security lapses.

Wendzel et al. [16] divide network covert storage channels into two categories: (i) techniques that change header fields or other non-payload elements and (ii) techniques

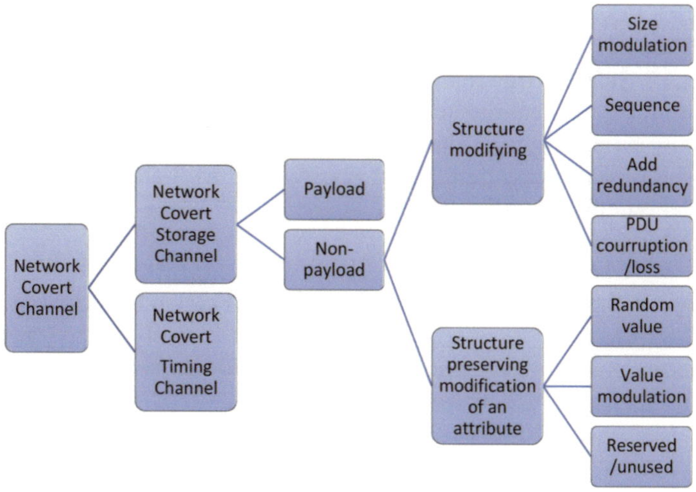

Figure 2.
Network covert channel classification.

that conceal covert messages into the payload section. Moreover, seven patterns are used to categorize the non-payload techniques. These seven categories include random value, add redundancy, sequence, size modulation, value modulation, and reserved/ unused. In terms of network covert timing channels, Wendzel et al. classified them into four categorization patterns that include retransmission, PDU order, rate, and inter-arrival time. **Figure 2** shows the classification of network covert channels.

4. Typical covert channel model

Simmons [21] described the prisoner's dilemma that serves as an example of a typical or common covert channel scenario.

Two prisoners named Alice and Bob want to talk to each other so that they may plot their escape. However, Wendy, a third party, keeps an eye on the potential

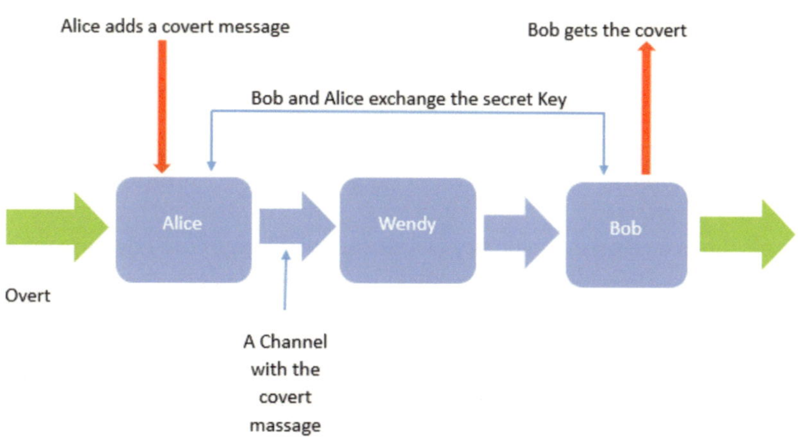

Figure 3.
Typical covert channel model.

communication channel between them. Alice and Bob will be placed in solitary confinement without the ability to share information if Wendy or the warden discovers any suspicious activity on this channel. In order to communicate covertly, Alice and Bob must attempt to conceal the information they transmit in a way that Wendy cannot discover. By supposing that Alice and Bob are communicating *via* two networked computers, this scenario may be adapted to network covert channels [22]. The covert channel model is depicted in **Figure 3**.

5. Factors behind the advanced development of covert channels

The following points are a summary of some significant elements that are crucial in the development of covert channel techniques [23]:

- The rapid advancement of cloud computing, virtualization technologies, communication protocols, data centers, and network technologies. This cutting-edge research offers a wealth of opportunities to create various covert channel strategies.

- Techniques known as switching that enable a covert channel to change how it appears inside a particular protocol or from one protocol to another. This technique helps in creating covert channels that are difficult to discover.

- Internal control protocol technology that offers a trustworthy and dependable channel of communication for a covert message. This method employs a micro protocol to provide dynamic routing and dependable communication to a covert message.

6. Covert channels and modern technology

This section discusses the prevalence of covert channels among modern technologies and how these modern technologies offer a rich environment for creating many scenarios of covert communication that can have both beneficial and detrimental effects.

Khulaidi et al. indicated that scholars are increasingly focused on the threat posed by covert channels. These channels have an impact on emerging technologies including smart grid, VoIP, IoT, LTE, and IoUT [24].

The development of covert channels has been facilitated by IoT applications and related new technologies. There are a lot of covert communication techniques that take use of IoT protocols.

Network interfaces on the majority of Internet of Things (IoT) devices make them publicly accessible. These devices are typical in that they lack proper security measures and have limited resources, including memory, computing power, and batteries. As a result, they can be taken advantage of by many kinds of assaults.

Tan et al. [25] provided evidence of how IoT settings are susceptible to covert timing channels. They examined five techniques to building covert time channels for the Internet of Things. These five channels are based on scheduling, packet loss, rate switching, packet reordering, retransmission, and packet switching. Each of these covert channels operates differently.

Message Queuing Telemetry Transport (MQTT) is a lightweight client–server message transport protocol that is particularly well-suited for machine-to-machine and Internet of Things (IoT) connectivity. It is appropriate for high-latency and low-bandwidth situations, push communications, enterprise backends to mobile communications, and devices with limited resources. MQTT version 5.0 was examined by Mileva et al. [26] to see if it could be exploited by covert channels. It was discovered that some features in this version might be used to set up several covert channels.

Numerous covert channels that exploit Constrained Application Protocol (CoAP) were presented in [27]. CoAP is a web transfer protocol that is utilized for constrained networks and devices. It is among the protocols that will be most frequently abused in the upcoming years.

This indicates the continued advancement of covert channels and their deployment capabilities despite the sophisticated development of network techniques, particularly the Internet of Things, which has evolved into a widely used communication platform.

Despite the fact that IoT security has been the subject of several studies, not much attention has been paid to assessing the potential effectiveness of the covert channels threat in IoT contexts [5].

Permissionless blockchain is a potential option for covert communication because it is an emerging network application with qualities like decentralization, immutability, anonymity, and security. Wide access, large capacity covert channels, information concealment and identity anonymity, and resilient communication channels are among the benefits of blockchain technology for covert communication. Zang et al. [2] investigated covert channels across several blockchain layers and identified six types of covert channels in contract layer, network layer, data layer, and motivation layer of blockchain. A great medium for covert communication is the blockchain network [28].

A framework for covert channels based on blockchain that attempts to get beyond censorship was proposed by [29]. The authors tested the functionality of a prototype system they had designed for their proposed covert channel. The prototype is durable, efficient, and unobservable, according to the results obtained as indicated by the authors.

By investigating twenty-two years of traffic, Żórawski et al. addressed the Internet's vulnerability to covert channels. Evidence suggests that the opportunities for setting up covert channels are many and have changed throughout time. One-fits-all solutions are not practical; thus, as part of ongoing cybersecurity monitoring, there should be a periodic quantification of the information that may be concealed in traffic [30].

7. Countermeasures

Merely safeguarding communication content is no longer enough to satisfy the present standards for information security. Traditional encryption approaches and physical layer security strategies try to stop eavesdropping on communication content. However, meeting the current standards for information security requires more than just safeguarding communication content. Certain sensitive information may still be leaked *via* metadata, such as network traffic patterns, even when the data is encrypted [31].

The ability to fully understand covert channel techniques is essential for developing countermeasures. Computer network communication technology is developing so quickly; therefore, it is not logical to try to fully eliminate or prove the nonexistence of all potential covert channels. Alternatively, techniques to reduce or deteriorate the bandwidth of such covert channels have been developed [32]; however, in those cases, it is important to maintain a balance to keep the overt channel functional while attempting to reduce the covert channel capacity. Common techniques for capacity reduction or bandwidth reduction include adding noise, inserting dummy packets, limiting host-to-host connections, and establishing a fixed size for network packet length [33].

The common countermeasures for covert channels include:

i. Elimination: the process to eliminate a covert channel such as normalization of a protocol headers.

ii. Limitation: the process of limiting a covert channel bandwidth such as applying random traffic padding techniques.

iii. Audit: the process of auditing a covert channel that requires a reliable passive warden as a detection approach.

iv. Documenting a covert channel.

The majority of suggested detection strategies rely on the identification of abnormal behavior. Since the warden often understands the normal traffic patterns within a given network, it may quickly identify unusual activity resulting from covert communication. Nevertheless, these methods are unable to identify hidden traffic if there are significant changes in the normal traffic. Furthermore, it will be challenging to identify any covert traffic that resembles regular traffic.

Caviglione [4] pointed out that future research indicates that covert channels will continue to be a popular model for stegomalware empowerment and data exfiltration, new assaults will likely be more complicated, cross-layer, and capable of using the intricate interactions between hardware and software. Due to ambiguity about what to check and where to position wardens within the broader network architecture, this enlarges the gap between attackers and defenders. Caviglione pointed out the key patterns in the development of countermeasures together with the challenges that need to be overcome as follows:

- Generalization: using a variety of collecting methods and inspecting many heterogeneous carriers may be necessary for data collection, network covert channel identification, and sanitization.

- Abstraction: one intriguing method is to provide more abstract measurements that can be utilized to identify the steganographic assault regardless of the carrier that is being employed. However, this may require further security measures that degrade the performance.

- Cloud: cloud infrastructures will continue to be an important part of the Internet of the future. Recent studies have shown how cloud designs may be used to provide pathways for communication *via* the Internet. Consequently, it is imperative to safeguard cloud and virtualized systems against attacks that might conceal information such as covert network channels.

- Everything-as-a-service: the detection of covert channels needs a significant amount of processing and storage capacity. For small- to medium-sized actors, it might not be possible to operate sophisticated detection software or deploy wardens to secure large-scale networks while still providing acceptable performance. Consequently, it might be advisable to investigate Warden-as-a-Service strategies.

- Reversibility: in case of reversible network covert channels, the warden should gather communications from various network segments and do some sort of comparison. This presents a number of challenges, including legal and technical matters.

- Resistance by design: ambiguous designs or imperfect implementations are typically the cause of the capacity to store arbitrary data or alter protocols. When creating network protocols, one should take into account the patterns that serve as the foundation for the establishment of covert channels. Another interesting trend to investigate is the use of formal methods to provide a warden the capacity to do runtime checks or model unexpected risks.

In light of this, Caviglione suggests that future studies concentrate on creating more comprehensive frameworks and indications as well as strategies for simultaneously inspecting several carriers. Although there is some evidence of this tendency in the literature, it has to be strengthened in order to be useful. Educating developers and engineers about the dangers posed by network coverts channels is another worthwhile avenue to explore.

Modern malware uses information hiding to evade detection and employ a variety of deceptive and hostile techniques. Developing covert channels is turning into one of the most effective ways to obtain more harmful payloads or exfiltrate confidential data. Notwithstanding their influence on Internet security, a clear assessment of network traffic's vulnerability to covert channels is lacking. Furthermore, in order to develop countermeasures, it is essential to comprehend how the targeted protocol and its diffusion drive the hiding capacity [30].

It is preferable for individuals who emphasis on developing covert channels for legitimate use to focus their efforts on identifying the exploited vulnerabilities that lead to the creation of covert channels rather than creating covert channels for beneficial purposes. In order to overcome flaws and vulnerabilities in the system architecture or other stages of security against the possibility of a covert channel, this would be very helpful [13].

8. Covert channel detection

Techniques for using covert channels have improved the ability to carry out risky and unobserved assaults. Because they take use of methods not meant for information transmission, they are invisible to conventional security procedures [34]. There is a challenge to identify, reduce, or remove them. Several research papers demonstrate the practical application of machine learning (ML) classification techniques for the identification of covert channels. Because ML and deep learning (DL) have great accuracy and precision, studies over the last 5 years have focused on identifying covert channel using ML and DL; nevertheless, the dataset has to be improved to facilitate training and testing [24].

This section examines the benefits and drawbacks of detection techniques mostly based on ML classification models, in which recent work has been given more attention.

The Internet's core protocols are TCP/IP suite. It involves the greatest number of protocols that might be exploited by attackers *via* covert channels. Compared to other fields, a covert channel that exploits ISN field of TCP protocol appears most difficult to discover [35]. To identify ISN covert channels, Sohn et al. [36] introduced a detection technique using support vector machine (SVM) classifier. However, their approach is time-consuming and requires a significant number of both normal and malicious ISNs traffic to be trained in order to effective in identifying covert attacks [37].

The majority of detection approaches to detect network covert channel concentrate on a particular type of covert channel technique rather than focusing on the shared characteristics of several different types of covert channels. In this context, Wendzel et al. [16] categorized covert channel approaches into eleven categories in an effort to develop a mechanism to identify common behaviors of covert channels. Wendzel et al. noted that almost 70% of these methods fall into four major categories. This result aids to introduce a common framework or common frameworks to be used to develop a common detection model that is capable to identify a group of covert channels instead of a applying a single model for each covert channel. This significantly reduces the security system overhead.

A detection method that uses hierarchy and density clusters was proposed by Yuwen et al. [38]. They stated that their detection technique could identify various kinds of covert channels and could also effectively discriminate between covert and normal traffic even at channel noise rates of up to 20%.

The simplest method for removing covert channels based on packet length is usually to equalize packet lengths to their maximum length. This can unquestionably prevent packet length covert channel; nonetheless, this approach lowers network capacity and is therefore seen as insufficient. In another method, covert channels packet lengths can be restricted by limiting the range of lengths that a packet can have. This reduces the number of states that a covert message may exploit, hence limiting the capacity of the covert channel. If a packet is too small, zeroes can be appended to it as padding. This method, however, consumes the bandwidth of the overt channel. Consequently, it remains a problem to find an efficient way to reduce or limit the capacity of covert channels without compromising the capacity of overt communication. In a recent study, Elsadig et al. [39] have noted that a popular area in network security is the use of ML approaches to detect different security threats, such as covert channel assaults. As a result, they provided an ensemble approach to identify packet length covert channels. Basing their work in the fact that ensemble approaches—which combine multiple classification methods in a manner that increases their benefits and reduces their weaknesses—can yield better results. The proposed ensemble approach combines the output of several classifiers using a stacking technique. Among these classifiers are Naive Bayes (NB), Random Forest (RF), and Support Vector Machine (SVM), whereas the output of these classifiers is aggregated by Logistic Regression (LR) classifier that acts as a meta-classifier for the proposed ensemble approach. According to the published results, the proposed ensemble approach outperformed the other individual classifiers that made up the approach in terms of accuracy. It performed better than all of them, detecting covert channels based on packet length with a 98.5% detection accuracy rate. Additionally, the proposed ensemble classifier performed well in terms of recall, accuracy, and specificity.

ML techniques function only in situations where there is some variance between covert and regular communication. As a result, the ML system either loses its ability to detect covert assaults or experiences a decline in detection accuracy when an attacker tries to imitate regular traffic.

An ML algorithm must be regularly taught to maintain its performance in order for it to monitor network live traffic and be successful. If not, the algorithm's efficiency will eventually decline. Classification models must be updated and retrained on a regular basis to withstand the fast growth of both overt and covert traffic. Periodic retraining, however, increases expense and degrades network speed and service quality. Elsadig et al. [40] looked at how effective ML techniques were at identifying covert channel assaults. They gave a succinct overview of covert channel assaults, emphasizing how emerging technologies like IPv6 protocol, IoT, and VoLTE frequently employ covert channel approaches. This demonstrates how these technologies are susceptible to covert channel assaults and how they offer a rich environment conducive to the development of a wide range of challenging covert channel attacks. Elsadig et al. investigated the benefits and drawbacks of ML classification methods for thwarting covert channel assaults. Their study reported that ML algorithms can successfully meet the demands of the modern security industry while also significantly assisting in the detection of covert channel assaults; however, they reported out some issues regarding using ML classifiers to identify covet channel as follows:

- For experimentation, several authors have created their own datasets; but they are not making them publicly available. Additionally, there are several issues with current datasets, including unevenness and outdated content.

- One important question about the datasets generated is how researchers verify that the regular traffic, upon which their study is based, is, in fact, overt traffic. It is likely that there is a type of covert channel that has not been discovered yet; thus, researchers need to use several traffic samples from different networks and circumstances to corroborate their results in order to create dependable normal traffic. That means validation of a dataset is highly required, which leads to reliable findings.

Due to overlapping within the time range of normal and abnormal network traffic, it will be challenging to distinguish between the two types of traffic in covert timing channels. This overlap may occur if the packet delay threshold used to hide a covert message is equivalent to or lower than 25% of the mean of inter-arrival time of the normal network traffic. If the double mean of inter-arrival time of normal traffic is reached or exceeded by the threshold, then the overlap will not occur, and therefore, covert traffic may be easily distinguished [41]. This illustrates how difficult it is to forecast covert timing channels with a packet delay threshold of at least 25% of the mean inter-arrival time of overt traffic. This suggests that developing suitable detection techniques for these kinds of situations would likely be more challenging [40].

An approach to identify covert timing channels was put out by Al-Eidi et al. [42]. Their method is made specifically to identify covert communications using ML and image processing. The traffic's inter-arrival times were transformed into colored images. In order to identify covert channels, a variety of ML classifiers were then trained using attributes that were taken from the colored images. Furthermore, the authors suggested a method for identifying the covert data inside a traffic flow, enabling the dropping of only the portion of the flow containing the covert message as opposed to the full flow. However, according to Ali [43], this method and the others described in [44, 45] primarily exploit the network flow's time information as a feature to identify covert timing channels that encrypt data using time. This indicates that an HTTP cookie covert channel that does not employ the time to encrypt information cannot be identified by these methods. Moreover, this approach is unreliable in cases where the behavior of a covert channel is marginally altered [46].

A stacking technique-based ensemble classification approach is introduced by [47]. Three classifiers were merged into this ensemble classifier: SVM, RF, and KNN. When compared to the techniques described in [48–51], the area under the curve (AUC) increased and reached 0.999, according to the authors. However, there is not enough indications to support the capacity of the proposed approach to identify even unknown covert or malicious traffic, despite its ability to identify two types of unknown traffic [40].

Han et al. [52] pointed out the drawbacks of a number of already available detection techniques that are intended to identify particular kinds of covert timing channels; as a result, they suggested a detection approach to address these problems. Their suggested model makes use of a KNN classifier that was trained using a number of statistical variables related to time intervals and payload lengths. Their scheme's AUC was 0.9737, and its accuracy rate was 0.96. To make sure their proposed scheme is capable to identify various CTCs, a variety of CTCs were put into practice. However, if attackers know the way to evade the statistical analysis of the covert channels, then the detection scheme may fail. Put otherwise, the detection technique breaks down when an attacker figures out how to get around the channel's statistical analysis. As a result, the extracted characteristics that are working well now could not work well in the future.

According to Wu et al. [53], there are three types of classic detection methods for CTCs: entropy-based, ML, and statistical-based methods. Ali summed up the drawbacks of the aforementioned techniques as follows:

- Less robustness: when there is none ideal network condition, for instance, jitter or packet loss, the detection accuracy of these approaches may deteriorate.
- Poor real-time performance: these techniques cannot identify CTCs quickly since they need more sampled inter-arrival times.
- Less universality: a couple of these techniques are limited to detecting a small number of distinct CTC types.

To get around these shortcomings. Wu et al. [53] proposed a time series symbolization-based detection technique for CTC identification. They convert inter-arrival times into symbolic representation using the k-Means clustering technique. Additionally, they proposed a method for calculating similarity that is based on the state transition probability model. The outcomes of their experiment demonstrated that, in optimal network conditions, the proposed detection approach may reach a 96% detection accuracy. While the proposed approach performs somewhat better than traditional approaches in the situation of existing network jitter, its performance also deteriorates noticeably with increasing network jitter.

Zillien and Wendzel [46] investigated two highly cited detection techniques: compressibility score [54] and ϵ -similarity [55]; both were proposed by Cabuk et al. Furthermore, two other new ML-based detection techniques, GAS [20] and SnapCatch [42], were examined. The authors pointed out that in the event that a covert channel behavior is marginally altered, these approaches are unreliable. Specifically, Zillien and Wendzel showed that all these detection techniques can be evaded or the performance may be drastically decreased when faced with a straightforward covert channel, named ϵ - κ libur, although the covert channel continues to provide a high bitrate.

Using a dataset that included both malicious traffic (packet length based covert channel) and valid traffic, the authors in [40] tested and trained eight different classification models, stack, decision tree (DT), K-nearest neighbors (KNN), support vector machine (SVM), logistic regression (LR), random forest (RF), neural network (NN), and naïve bayes (NB), to examine the best model in identifying packet length covert channel. The authors categorized these classifiers into four groups, poor, moderate good, and very good, based on their findings. With very good accuracy rates over 97.5%, Stack, NB, NN, and LR outperformed the good group that includes RF and SVM. They both attained accuracy rates of 96.4% and 96.9%. The DT earned a reasonable (moderate) accuracy that reached 88.3%, while the KNN classifier lagged behind with a poor accuracy rating of 68.6%.

Sattolo [56] proposed a detection method using LR classifier to identify a covert channel that exploits ID field of the IP protocol. Their method obtained a remarkable accuracy rate to identify the aforementioned IP covert channel. However, this detection method is effective for a simple covert channel.

9. Discussion

Modern advancements in computer network and intrusion detection system (IDS) technologies enable hackers to come up with new strategies for surreptitiously leaking private data. It is argued that two users are speaking covertly or indirectly when a communication between them, or between processes acting on their behalf, violates the interpretation of a security model set by a system. A covert channel is any communication route that might be utilized by a process to transfer data in a manner that is prohibited by a system's security policy. Vulnerabilities in network protocols are a source of hidden channel abuse.

Covert channel technology has emerged as a cutting-edge technique that presents several security techniques such as cybercrime evidence, network authentication, copyright protection, and so forth. However, it would be preferable to focus on identifying the weaknesses that are subject to be exploited to create a covert attack rather than creating covert channels for beneficial purposes.

A deep comprehension of covert channel strategies and techniques is necessary to develop countermeasures for covert channels. Owing to the complexity and the advanced growth of the technology of networking and communication, seeking to completely eliminate any possible hidden channels or demonstrating their nonexistence is irrational.

It is critically necessary to put more effort to introduce alternate solutions, for instance, lowering a covert channel capacity, inspecting a covert channel, recording covert channel, and so on. Furthermore, when reducing channel bandwidth, the solution should maintain the capacity for normal traffic while reducing the bandwidth of the channel.

The effectiveness of ML algorithms to thwart covert channel assaults was explored in this chapter, with a particular emphasis on their advantages and disadvantages. The analysis concludes that ML algorithms can effectively address present security needs in the real world and play a significant role in detecting covert channel attacks. However, when ML algorithms are used to mimic regular traffic, they either become less accurate in detecting covert channels or fail to identify them at all. Furthermore, there are several flaws in ML algorithms that let attackers launch complex assaults. Consequently, it is essential to evaluate ML technique vulnerabilities early in the development process in order to counter such attacks.

It is not feasible to have a different solution for each kind of covert channel as this might result in increasing overhead for network capacity and performance, which would lower quality of service (QoS). The majority of the detection techniques now in use are restricted to identifying particular kinds of covert channels and cannot be expanded to include more covert channels.

As a result, it is strongly advised to build multi-detection techniques that can identify many kinds of hidden channels. But as with multi-detection systems, creating such approaches calls for careful design to guarantee a high detection accuracy rate with low overheads.

Most recommended detection techniques are predicated on identifying abnormal behavior. Given its familiarity with the normal traffic patterns inside a network, the warden can detect unexpected behavior that may be the result of covert communication. However, if there are notable variations in the normal traffic, these techniques are unable to detect covert traffic. It will also be difficult to spot any covert traffic that looks like normal traffic.

Despite the fact that IoT security has been the subject of several studies, not much attention has been paid to assessing the potential effectiveness of the covert channels threat in IoT contexts. Generally, designers and developers should take into consideration in early phases the weaknesses that can be exploited by covert channel attacks.

10. Conclusion

A network covert channel provides an open avenue for hackers to spread destructive activity or leak private information without being discovered. An overview of covert channel concepts, techniques, classifications, and countermeasures is provided in this chapter, with a focus on how new technologies are often used to create covert channel assaults. This shows how they provide a rich setting for developing such attacks. This chapter provides an extensive overview of popular covert channel detection, emphasizing machine learning-based detection techniques for enhanced concentration. In addition, this chapter gives a through comprehensive investigation on the common countermeasure techniques that include elimination, limitation, detection, auditing, and documentation with a focus on their advantages and limitations. Even while several studies have shown that hidden channels can be advantageous and have emerged as a cutting-edge technique, this chapter emphases on covert channels as a threat that compromise our data and networks. There has been a thorough discussion on the risks associated with covert channels and the extent to which developers, designers, and security experts must work together to overcome any potential weaknesses than can be exploited to commit covert channel attacks.

Conflict of interest

No conflict of interest.

DOI: http://dx.doi.org/10.5772/intechopen.1005053

Author details

Muawia Elsadig
Imam Abdulrahman Bin Faisal University, Damma, KSA

*Address all correspondence to: muawiasadig66@gmail.com

References

[1] Miketic I, Dhananjay K, Salman E. Covert channel communication as an emerging security threat in 2.5D/3D integrated systems. Sensors. 2023;**23**(4). DOI: 10.3390/s23042081

[2] Zhang T, Li B, Zhu Y, Han T, Wu Q. Covert channels in blockchain and blockchain based covert communication: Overview, state-of-the-art, and future directions. Computer Communications. 2023;**205**:136-146. DOI: 10.1016/j.comcom.2023.04.001

[3] Elsadig MA, Fadlalla YA. Packet length covert channels crashed. Journal of Computer Science & Computational Mathematics. 2018;**8**(4):59-66. DOI: 10.20967/jcscm.2018.04.001

[4] Caviglione L. Trends and challenges in network covert channels countermeasures. Applied Sciences. 2021;**11**(4). DOI: 10.3390/app11041641

[5] Cabaj K, Żórawski P, Nowakowski P, Purski M, Mazurczyk W. Efficient distributed network covert channels for Internet of things environments. Journal of Cybersecurity. 2020;**6**(1):tyaa018

[6] Makhdoom I, Abolhasan M, Lipman J. A comprehensive survey of covert communication techniques, limitations and future challenges. Computers & Security. 2022;**120**:102784. DOI: 10.1016/j.cose.2022.102784

[7] Elsadig MA, Fadlalla YA. Survey on covert storage channel in computer network protocols: Detection and mitigation techniques In: Proceedings of the International Conference on Advances in Information Processing and Communication Technology - IPCT 2016, Rome, Italy. 2016. pp. 79-85. DOI: 10.15224/ 978-1-63248-099-6-71

[8] Ying X, Bernieri G, Conti M, Poovendran R. TACAN: Transmitter authentication through covert channels in controller area networks. In: Proceedings of the 10th ACM/IEEE International Conference on Cyber-Physical Systems, Montreal, QC, Canada. 2019. pp. 23-34. DOI: 10.1145/3302509.3313783

[9] Vanderhallen S, Van Bulck J, Piessens F, Mühlberg JT. Robust authentication for automotive control networks through covert channels. Computer Networks. 2021;**193**:108079

[10] Xie H, Zhao J. A lightweight identity authentication method by exploiting network covert channel. Peer-to-Peer Networking and Applications. 2015;**8**(6):1038-1047

[11] Elsadig MA, Fadlalla YA. An efficient approach to resolving packet length covert channels. In: 6th International Conference on Computer Engineering and Mathematical Sciences, Lankawi, Malaysia. 2017

[12] Lampson BW. A note on the confinement problem. Communications of the ACM. 1973;**16**(10):613-615

[13] Elsadig MA, Fadlalla YA. Network protocol covert channels: Countermeasures techniques. In: 2017 9th IEEE-GCC Conference and Exhibition (GCCCE); Manama, Bahrain; 8-11 May 2017. 2017. pp. 1-9. DOI: 10.1109/IEEEGCC.2017.8447997

[14] Hammouda S, Maalej L, Trabelsi Z. Towards optimized TCP/IP covert channels detection, IDS and firewall integration. In: 2008 New Technologies, Mobility and Security, Tangier, Morocco, 5-7 November 2008. 2008. pp. 1-5. DOI: 10.1109/NTMS.2008.ECP.101

[15] Dakhane DM, Deshmukh PR. Active warden for TCP sequence number base covert channel. In: 2015 International Conference on Pervasive Computing (ICPC), Pune, India, 8-10 January 2015. 2015. pp. 1-5. DOI: 10.1109/PERVASIVE.2015.7087183

[16] Wendzel S, Zander S, Fechner B, Herdin C. Pattern-based survey and categorization of network covert channel techniques. ACM Computing Surveys (CSUR). 2015;**47**(3):50

[17] Elsadig MA, Fadlalla YA. A balanced approach to eliminate packet length-based covert channels. In: 2017 4th IEEE International Conference on Engineering Technologies and Applied Sciences (ICETAS), Salmabad, Bahrain, 29 November - 1 December 2017. 2017. pp. 1-7. DOI: 10.1109/ICETAS.2017.8277839

[18] Tian J, Xiong G, Li Z, Gou G. A survey of key technologies for constructing network covert channel. Security and Communication Networks. 2020;**2020**:1-20. DOI: 10.1155/2020/8892896

[19] Bedi P, Jindal V, Dua A. SPYIPv6: Locating covert data in one or a combination of IPv6 header field(s). IEEE Access. 2023;**11**:103486-103501. DOI: 10.1109/ACCESS.2023.3318172

[20] Li H, Song T, Yang Y. Generic and sensitive anomaly detection of network covert timing channels. IEEE Transactions on Dependable and Secure Computing. 2023;**20**(5):4085-4100. DOI: 10.1109/TDSC.2022.3207573

[21] Simmons GJ. The prisoners' problem and the subliminal channel. In: Advances in Cryptology. Vol. 1984. Boston, MA: Springer US; 22 Aug 1984. pp. 51-67

[22] Handel TG, Sandford MT. Hiding data in the OSI network model. In: Information Hiding. Berlin Heidelberg: Springer; 1996. pp. 23-38. DOI: 10.1007/3-540-61996-8_29

[23] Elsadig MA, Fadlalla YA. Packet length covert channel: A detection scheme. In: 2018 1st International Conference on Computer Applications & Information Security (ICCAIS), Riyadh, Saudi Arabia, 4-6 April 2018. 2018. pp. 1-7. DOI: 10.1109/CAIS.2018.8442026

[24] Khulaidi NAA, Zahary AT, Hazaa MAS, Nasser AA. Covert channel detection and generation techniques: A survey. In: 2023 3rd International Conference on Emerging Smart Technologies and Applications (eSmarTA), Taiz, Yemen, 10-11 October 2023. 2023. pp. 01-09. DOI: 10.1109/eSmarTA59349.2023.10293582

[25] Tan Y-A, Zhang X, Sharif K, Liang C, Zhang Q, Li Y. Covert timing channels for IoT over mobile networks. IEEE Wireless Communications. 2018;**25**(6):38-44

[26] Mileva A, Velinov A, Hartmann L, Wendzel S, Mazurczyk W. Comprehensive analysis of MQTT 5.0 susceptibility to network covert channels. Computers & Security. 2021;**104**:102207

[27] Mileva A, Velinov A, Stojanov D. New covert channels in Internet of Things. In: the 12th International Conference on Emerging Security Information, Systems and Technologies - SECURWARE 2018, Venice, Italy, September 16-20, 2018. 2018. pp. 30-36

[28] Zhang P, Cheng Q, Zhang M, Luo X. A blockchain-based secure covert communication method via Shamir threshold and STC mapping. IEEE Transactions on Dependable and Secure Computing. 2024:1-12. DOI: 10.1109/

TDSC.2024.3353570. Available from: https://ieeexplore.ieee.org/abstract/document/10398427

[29] Chen Z, Zhu L, Jiang P, Zhang C, Gao F, Guo F. Exploring unobservable blockchain-based covert channel for censorship-resistant systems. IEEE Transactions on Information Forensics and Security. 2024;**19**:3380-3394. DOI: 10.1109/TIFS.2024.3361212

[30] Żórawski P, Caviglione L, Mazurczyk W. A long-term perspective of the internet susceptibility to covert channels. IEEE Communications Magazine. 2023;**61**(10):171-177. DOI: 10.1109/MCOM.011.2200744

[31] Qiao S, Zhu R, Ji X, Zhao J, Ding H. Optimization of covert communication in multi-sensor asymmetric Noise systems. Sensors. 2024;**24**(3). DOI: 10.3390/s24030796

[32] Zander S, Armitage G, Branch P. A survey of covert channels and countermeasures in computer network protocols. Communications Surveys & Tutorials, IEEE. 2007;**9**(3):44-57

[33] Elsadig MA, Fadlalla YA. Survey on covert storage channel in computer network protocols: Detection and mitigation techniques. International Journal of Advances in Computer Networks and Its Security. 2016;**6**(3):11-17

[34] Elsadig MA, Gafar A. An ensemble model to detect packet length covert channels. International Journal of Electrical & Computer Engineering. 2023;**13**(5):5296-5304. DOI: 10.11591/ijece.v13i5.pp5296-5304

[35] Zhao H, Shi Y. Q. A phase-space reconstruction approach to detect covert channels in TCP/IP protocols. In: 2010 IEEE International Workshop on Information Forensics and Security. Seattle, WA, USA, 12-15 December 2010. 2010. pp. 1-6. DOI: 10.1109/WIFS.2010.5711441

[36] Sohn T, Seo J, Moon J. A study on the covert channel detection of TCP/IP header using support vector machine. In: Information and Communications Security. Berlin, Heidelberg: Springer; 2003. pp. 313-324. DOI: 10.1007/978-3-540-39927-8_29

[37] Elsadig MA. Resolving network packet length covert channels. [Ph.D. dissertation] Computer Science and Technology. Sudan: Sudan University of Science & Technology; 2018

[38] Yuwen Q, Huaju S, Chao S, Xi W, Linjie L. Network covert channel detection with cluster based on hierarchy and density. Procedia Engineering. 2012;**29**:4175-4180

[39] Elsadig M, Gafar A. Packet length covert channel detection: An ensemble machine learning approach. Journal of Theoretical and Applied Information Technology. 2022;**100**(23):7035-7043

[40] Elsadig MA, Gafar A. Covert channel detection: Machine learning approaches. IEEE Access. 2022;**10**:38391-38405. DOI: 10.1109/ACCESS.2022.3164392

[41] Qu H, Cheng Q, Yaprak E. Using covert channel to resist DoS attacks in WLAN. In: Proceedings of the 2005 International Conference on Wireless Networks, ICWN 2005, Las Networks. Vegas, Nevada, USA, June 27-30, 2005. 2005. pp. 38-44

[42] Al-Eidi S, Darwish O, Chen Y, Husari G. SnapCatch: Automatic detection of covert timing channels using image processing and machine learning. IEEE Access. 2021;**9**:177-191. DOI: 10.1109/ACCESS.2020.3046234

[43] Yuan W, Chen X, Zhu Y, Zeng X, Yue Y. HTTP cookie covert channel detection based on session flow interaction features. Security and Communication Networks. 2023;**2023**:1348393. DOI: 10.1155/2023/1348393

[44] Al-Eidi S, Darwish O, Chen Y. Covert timing channel analysis either as cyber attacks or confidential applications. Sensors. 2020;**20**(8). DOI: 10.3390/s20082417

[45] Darwish O, Al-Fuqaha A, Ben Brahim G, Jenhani I, Vasilakos A. Using hierarchical statistical analysis and deep neural networks to detect covert timing channels. Applied Soft Computing. 2019;**82**:105546. DOI: 10.1016/j.asoc.2019.105546

[46] Zillien S, Wendzel S. Weaknesses of popular and recent covert channel detection methods and a remedy. IEEE Transactions on Dependable and Secure Computing. 2023;**20**(6):5156-5167. DOI: 10.1109/TDSC.2023.3241451

[47] Yang P, Wan X, Shi G, Qu H, Li J, Yang L. Identification of DNS covert channel based on stacking method. International Journal of Computer and Communication Engineering. 2021;**10**(2):1-15

[48] Nadler A, Aminov A, Shabtai A. Detection of malicious and low throughput data exfiltration over the DNS protocol. Computers & Security. 2019;**80**:36-53

[49] Shafieian S, Smith D, Zulkernine M. Detecting DNS tunneling using ensemble learning. Cham: Springer; 2017. pp. 112-127. DOI: 10.1007/978-3-319-64701-2_9

[50] Karasaridis A, Meier-Hellstern K, Hoein D. Detection of DNS anomalies using flow data analysis, global telecommunications conference, 2006. In: GLOBECOM'06. IEEE; 2006

[51] Farnham G, Atlasis A. Detecting DNS tunneling. SANS Institute InfoSec Reading Room. 2013;**9**:1-32

[52] Han J, Huang C, Shi F, Liu J. Covert timing channel detection method based on time interval and payload length analysis. Computers & Security. 2020;**97**:101952

[53] Wu S, Chen Y, Tian H, Sun C. Detection of covert timing channel based on time series symbolization. IEEE Open Journal of the Communications Society. 2021;**2**:2372-2382

[54] Cabuk S. Network covert channels: Design, analysis, detection, and elimination [Ph.D.]. United States -- Indiana, 3260014: Purdue University; 2006. [Online]. Available from: https://library.iau.edu.sa/dissertations-theses/network-covert-channels-design-analysis-detection/docview/305285689/se-2?accountid=136546; http://by7nn3rg6h.search.serialssolutions.com/?genre=article&sid=ProQ:&atitle=Network+covert+channels:+Design,+analysis,+detection,+and+elimination&title=Network+covert+channels:+Design,+analysis,+detection,+and+elimination&issn=&date=2006-01-01&volume=&issue=&spage=&author=Cabuk,+Serdar

[55] Cabuk S, Brodley CE, Shields C. IP covert timing channels: Design and detection. In: Proceedings of the 11th ACM Conference on Computer and Communications Security, Washington, DC, USA, October 25-29, 2004. 2004. pp. 178-187. DOI: 10.1145/1030083.1030108

[56] Sattolo TAV. Real-time detection of storage covert channels. [Ph.D. dissertation] Department of Systems and Computer Engineering. Ottawa, Canada: Carleton University; 2021